THE WORLD SPA DESIGN II

ARTPOWER

THE WORLD SPA DESIGN II

ARTPOWER™

Designer: Chen Ting
Chief Editor: Xia Jiajia

Address: Room C, 9/F., Sun House , 181 Des Voeux Road Central,
Hong Kong, China
Tel: 852 3184 0676
Fax: 852 2543 2396

Editorial Department
G009, Floor 7th, Yimao Centre, Meiyuan Road, Luohu District,
Shenzhen, China
Tel: 86-755-82913355
Fax: 86-755-82020029

URL: www.artpower.com.cn
E-mail: artpower@artpower.com.cn

ISBN 978-988-16688-2-0

Printed in China

Preface

Saying wellness today risks appearing as a marketing operation, a term behind which often, softened by an aura of health consciousness and positivity, lurks in reality one of the largest consumer industries in history.

More often than not it has been and is just so, with the complicity – more or less aware – of an army of architects and designers, committed to dressing and to formally connoting precise and well codified commercial activities, rather than contributing to recreating "healthy" environments in the real sense of the term, capable of transmitting positivity and wellbeing ever through a wise use of architectonic space, shape, materials and colours, that is through a cultivated and sensitive creativity. The recent productive intensification of the industry aimed at materials and decorative products dedicated to this sector – ceramics, mosaics, enamelled glass and imitative artificial materials in general – all having their own aesthetic image of immediate application, if on one hand they enhance an indispensable repertory of products, on the other all they do is confirm a widespread orientation of designers towards the "pret à porter", demonstrating a clear predisposition to speculation and stylistic conformism rather than to pure research.

Even in this field some designers have never separated a profound commitment to formal research and the use of materials from the principle of uniqueness and originality of a project, believing that even that of wellness is a space of welcoming par excellence, different from others for a fundamental feature: every choice, from the architectonic project to the materials, from the lighting to the colours – even though sometimes congenial to particular treatments - must strike psychological and emotive aspects directly ascribable to wellbeing in a strict sense, in a measure that goes beyond the same activities that are done there. Furthermore, the creations illustrated here highlight how often it is not necessary to make use of specific commercial products, but instead how a sincere and emphatic, almost brutal but always harmonised use of traditional and conventional materials, may – thanks to their intrinsic naturalness and beauty – contribute efficaciously to attainment of that positive feeling and that sensation of psychological pleasure, that are the ideal prerequisite to spend a day of relaxation in a SPA.

Marco de Jorio

Contents

Aquagranda Livigno Wellness Park

Simone Micheli

Client: Aquagranda
Locationn: Livigno, Italy
Photography: Juergen Eheim
Area: 21,000 m^2

Aquagranda Livigno Wellness Park is conceived as a masterpiece space where both the physical and spiritual senses are commemorated, thus permitting the visitor to live emotionally relaxing experiences and psycho-physical regeneration. The perceptual experiences are ensured to be instantaneously transformed in wonderful memory. Covering

baby village
beauty centre
reception
dressing rooms
thermarium
garages

FLOOR 1

room's reception
commercial centre
bar-restaurant
black pool

FLOOR 2

rooms
bar

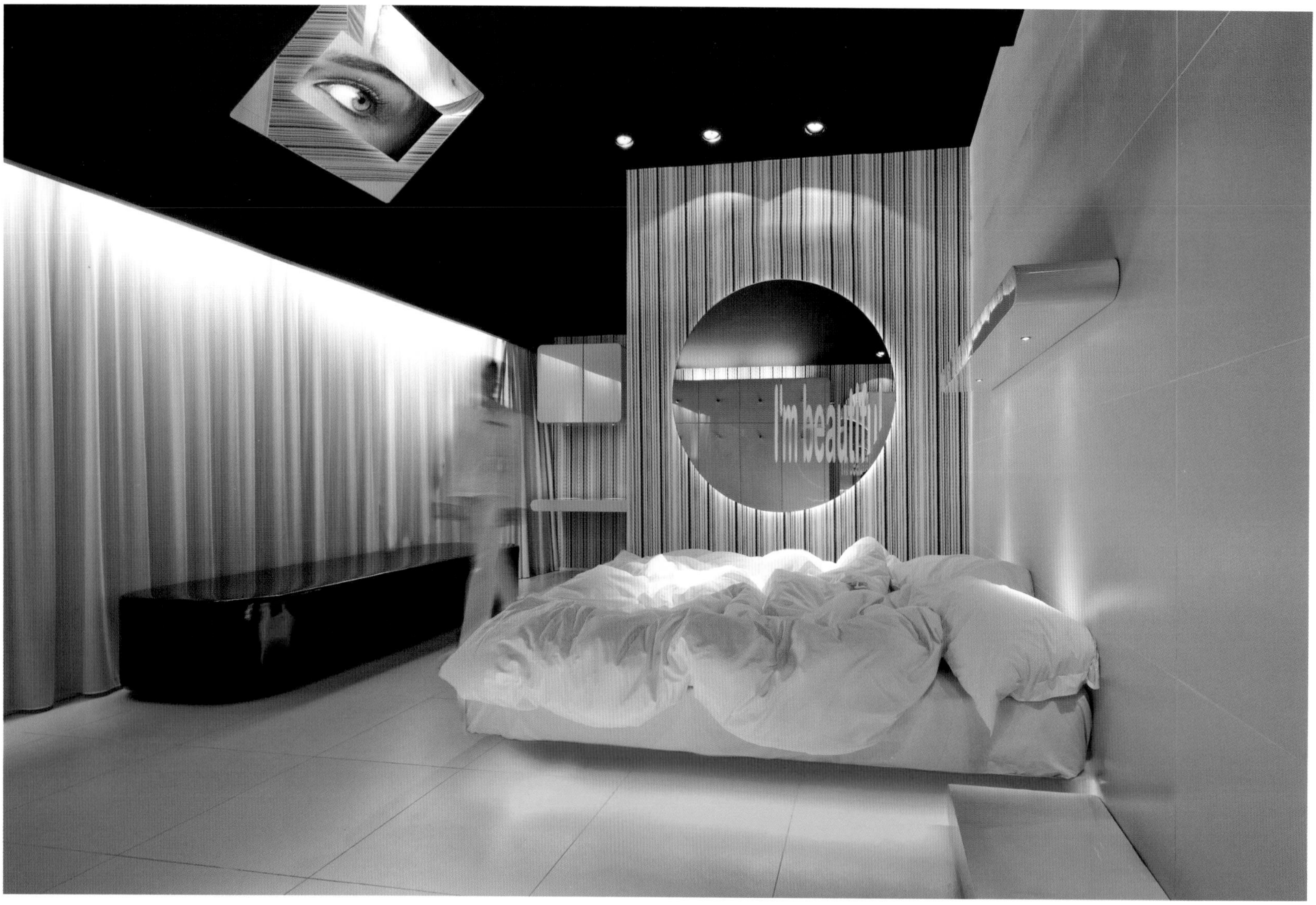
I'm beautiful

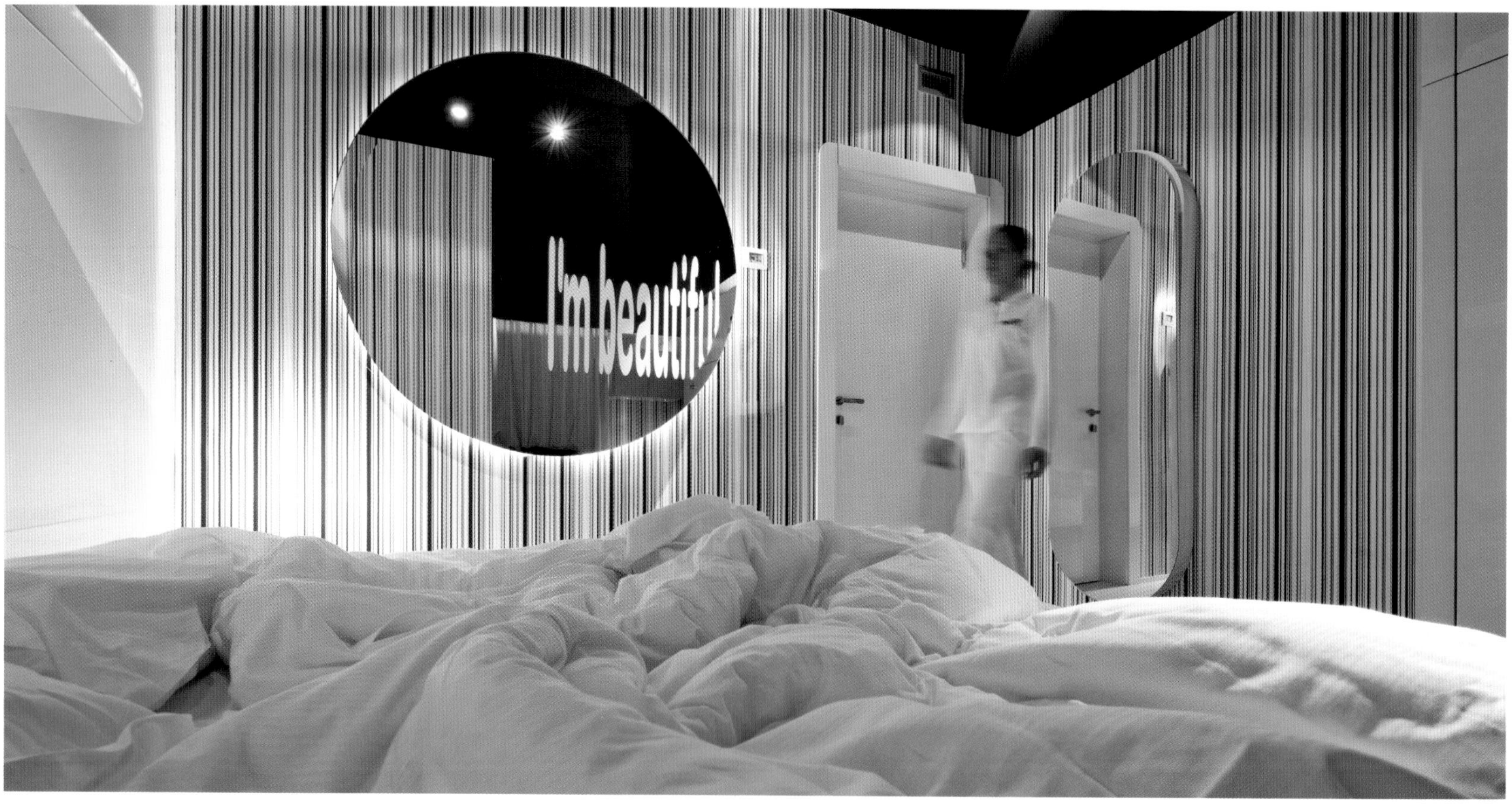
I'm beautiful

an area of around 21,000 square meters, the new complex integrates a large Spa; a wide beauty area dedicated to various body treatments and inhalations; various relaxing pools; a semi Olympic swimming pool; a fitness area; relax areas; commercial centre; restaurant; bar and a guest area structured to support the new wellness tourism. Based upon the simplicity and immediacy of a gesture, the project takes life thanks to the use of colours and basic yet absolutely functional furniture designed in fluid plastic shapes. It is an interactive exciting, hybrid, location, strongly characterized by environments and functions that integrate and oppose one another, identifying a path for celebrating the relation between men, built space and wellness; between climbing theories and compositional truths; between matter, surfaces, lights, colour, sound and finally water. Everything is designed to cradle the guest in this dream. In an unexpectedly black environment a gorgeous pool marked by water twirls and hydro massage is highlighted by the soft lighting, an equally unusual semi Olympic swimming pool submerges in a box dematerialized by absolute white colour and by some bright graphics. Saunas, Turkish baths, ham am, relaxing pools, thalassic therapy pools, cold environment and aromatic shower, lighting effect and videos projection on the walls animate the spa, conceived as an empty canvas on which the visitor plays an interactive role. The elegance, rigor and theatrical plastic scenery offered by the infinite vertigo characterise the aesthetics. Finally the guest area: with aggressive rooms in a conceptual yet practical design, dominated by the overlapping contrast of bright white and black tones.

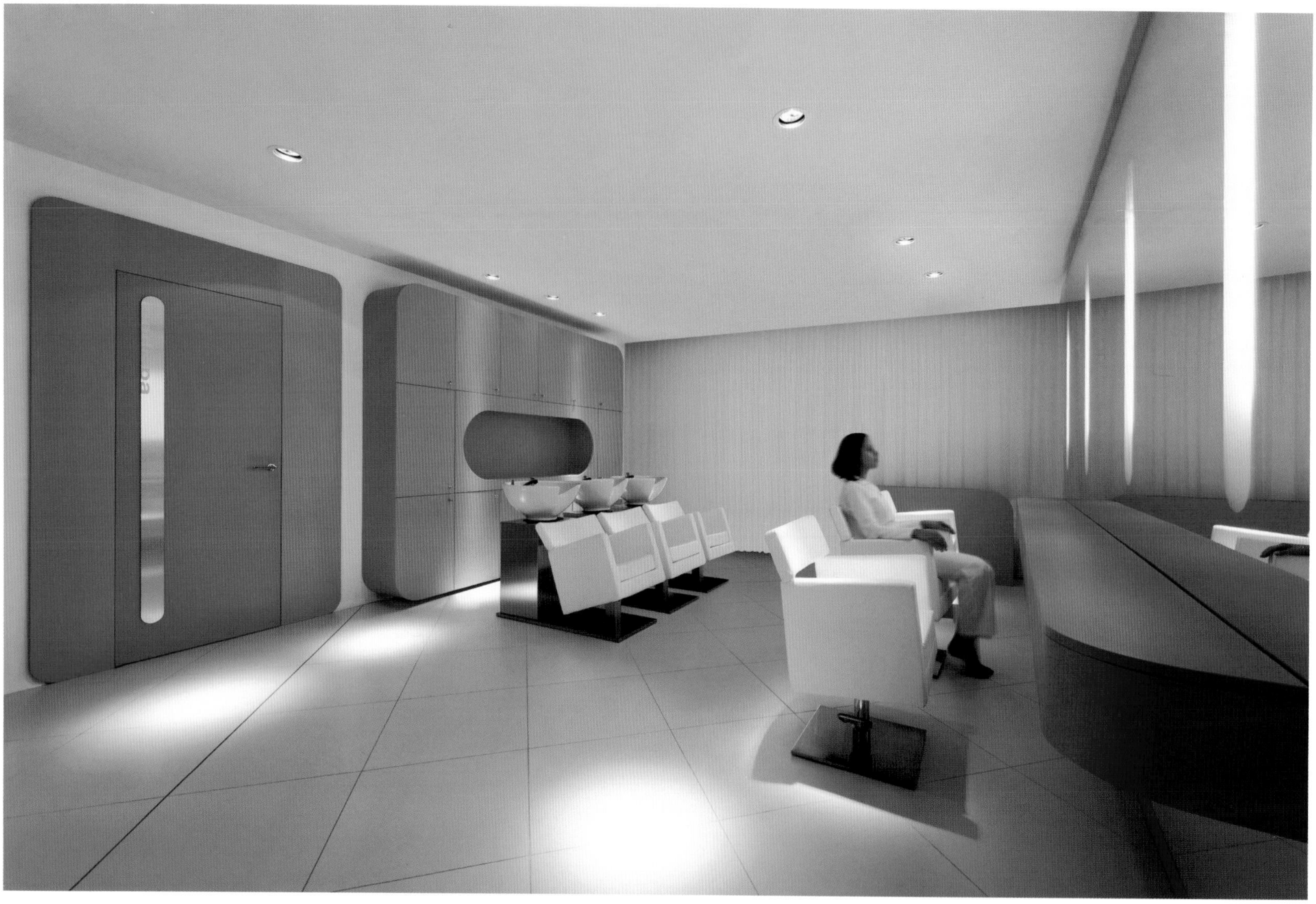

Wellness Center "Incontro"

Simone Micheli

Client: Mioblu Special Wellness
Location: Hotel Incontro, Ariano Irpino (AV), Italy
Photography: Juergen Eheim

The interior design project, entrusted to Architect Simone Micheli and to his wise interpretation of sensorial stimulation, is characterized as a modern health club. An emotional location able to involve and surprise, inviting the viewer to listen carefully in order to abandon fears and preconceptions.The result is an unbelievable multi-sensorial environment: stunning intensive brightness in one hand, relaxing pathways filled with rarefied atmosphere on the other hand. Thus becoming an emotional vehicle between physical and mental experience, external reality and inner world."Ethics and beauty are able to bring renewed oxygen to the life of contemporary man through contents and expressions". With these words and through his design, Architect Micheli aims to create a great space with strong content of signs.Regeneration and oxygenation of the senses, thus "Magical words" transcending the rational, relieving stress and rediscovering an inner part of oneself hidden by haste and those impenetrable moments of modern life. The SPA narrates and becomes a warm and friendly place, with innovative soft lines affected by unreal and unknown shapes. Bright colours are obtained with the use of meticulous and soft lightening, making the designed objects alive and interactive.

The visitor will enjoy this unrepeatable, deep and sin-aesthetic experience and will only gain energetic and intense emotions that will enable him to cross the threshold of the unknown and permit him to find a world with high aesthetic values of the body, mind and soul.

In a unique and visionary synthesis, the result is a spatial area built as an interactive, hybrid, emotional location, with environments and functions perfectly integrated with each other, contrasting with the surfaces, sounds and water and a contamination of multiple destinations connected to wellness.

spa
incontro

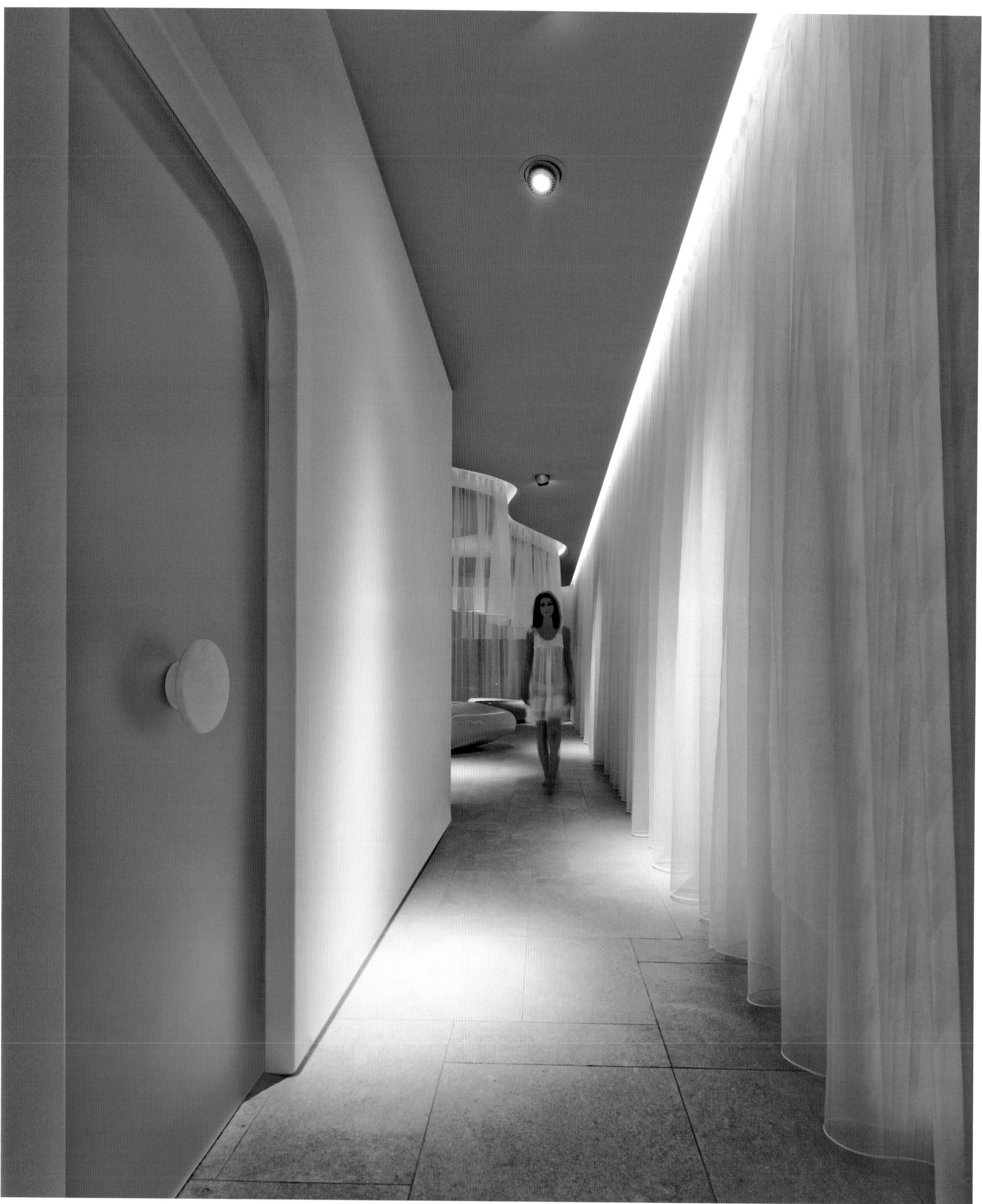

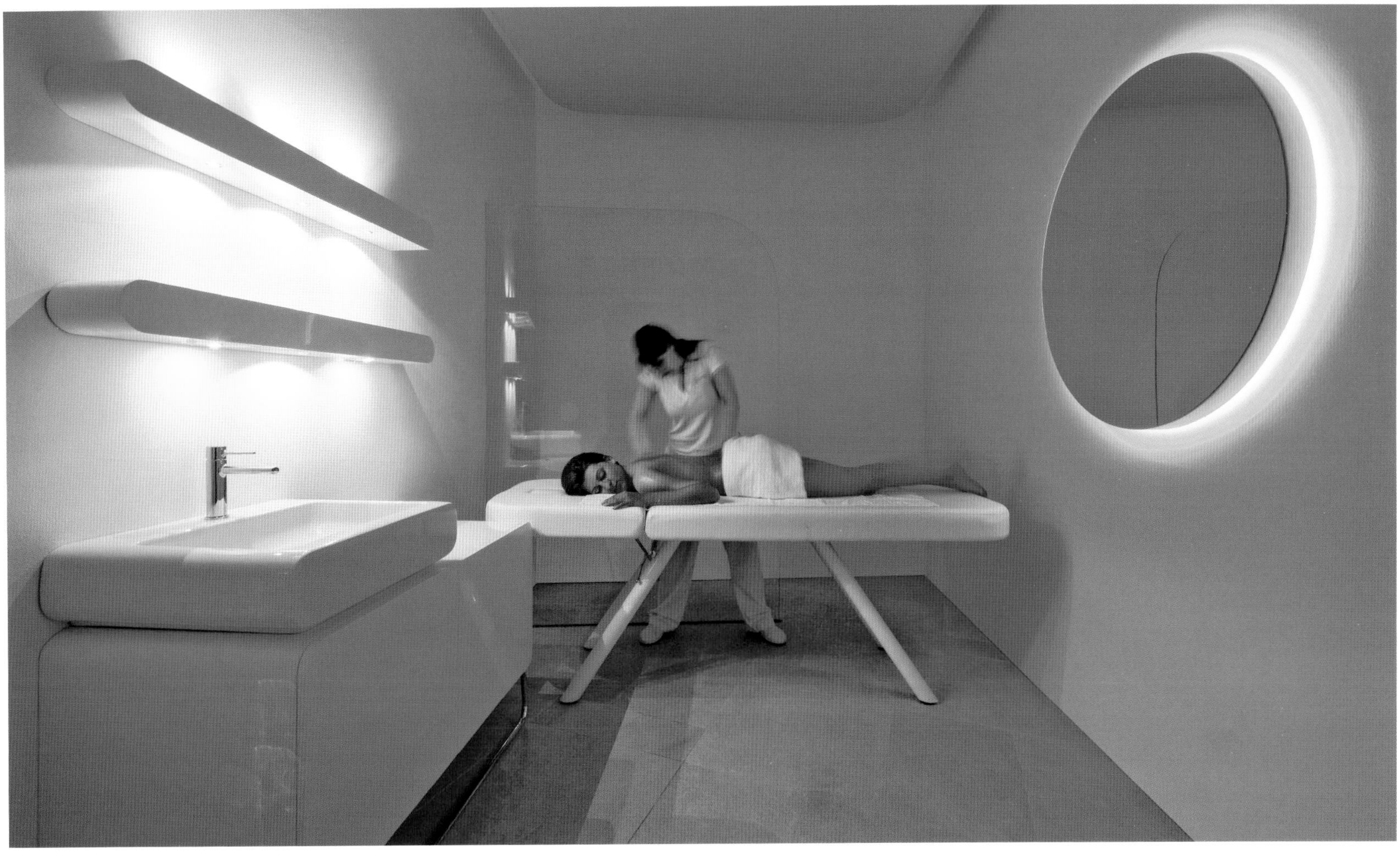

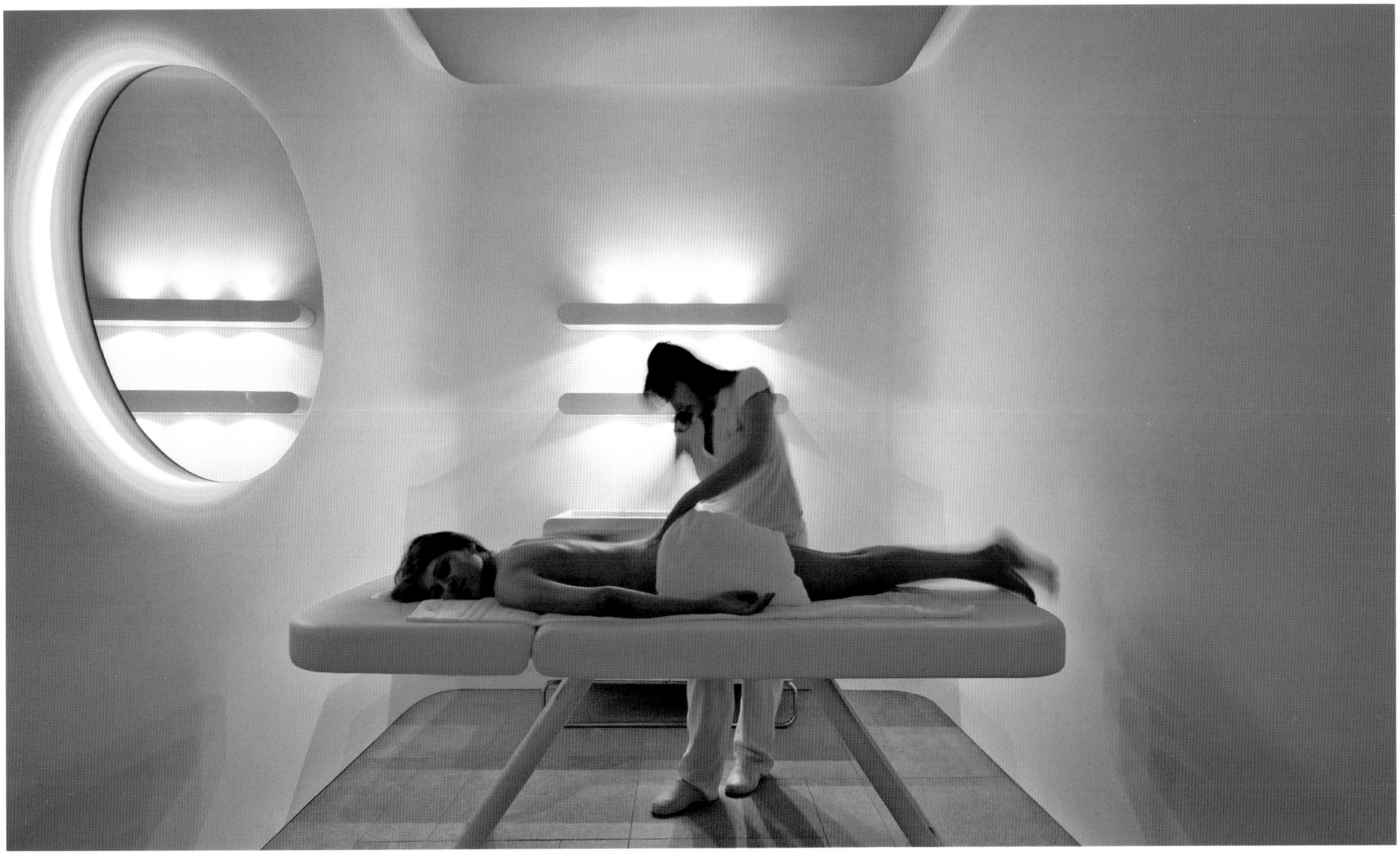

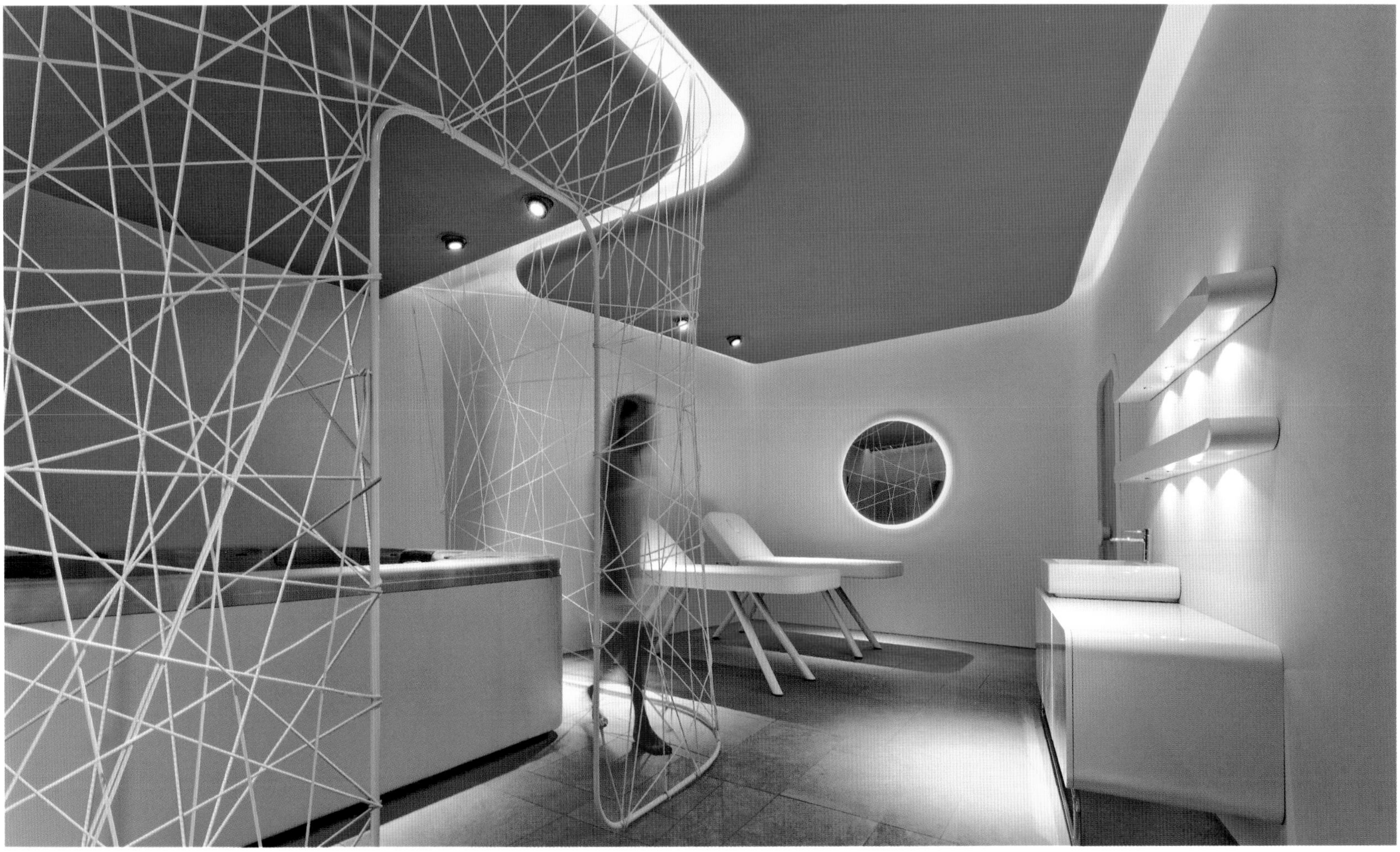

Terme Alte di Rivisondoli — Surreal Naturalness

Simone Micheli

Location: Località La Difesa, Rivisondoli (AQ), Italy
Area: 900 m²
Photography: Juergen Eheim

The dream of Architect Simone Micheli has taken shape and become reality at 1300 m. above sea level. Terme Alte di Rivisondoli, a recently opened spa and wellness facility, expresses excitement, rigor and simplicity. Fully integrated with the wild nature of the Abruzzo mountains — still little known despite their rare beauty — Terme Alte is a project not only of aesthetic refinement, but also of intelligence and strategic design and communication.

Set in a natural corner equidistant from the tourist centers of Roccaraso, Rivisondoli and Pescocostanzo, thanks to the expressive power of its spaces and the high quality of the treatments it offers, this oasis of relaxation aspires to become a major attraction, a means for energizing, enlivening and invigorating the handsome plateau it overlooks, the ski resorts of the surrounding mountains, the nearby golf courses and equestrian club, and the cycle hiking paths and that wind through the woods that surround it on three sides. Here Micheli has transformed his vision into a project of excellence and acumen. Exemplary in its approach, it reaches beyond the concept of eco-logical and eco-nomic sustainability, taking as its aim not a seemingly satisfying balance of the status quo, but the enrichment of the territory itself, the enhancement of the natural and human resources that are there.

Terme Alte di Rivisondoli is a place of architectural spells and charms as well, poised between the surreal and the dreamlike: lighting effects, scents, colors, transparencies and improbable geometries characterize this threedimensional realm suspended between dream and reality — effects by which we humans can be stimulated synaesthetically, and our visit, our use and enjoyment of the spaces, given a sense of unicity.

uom

acqua

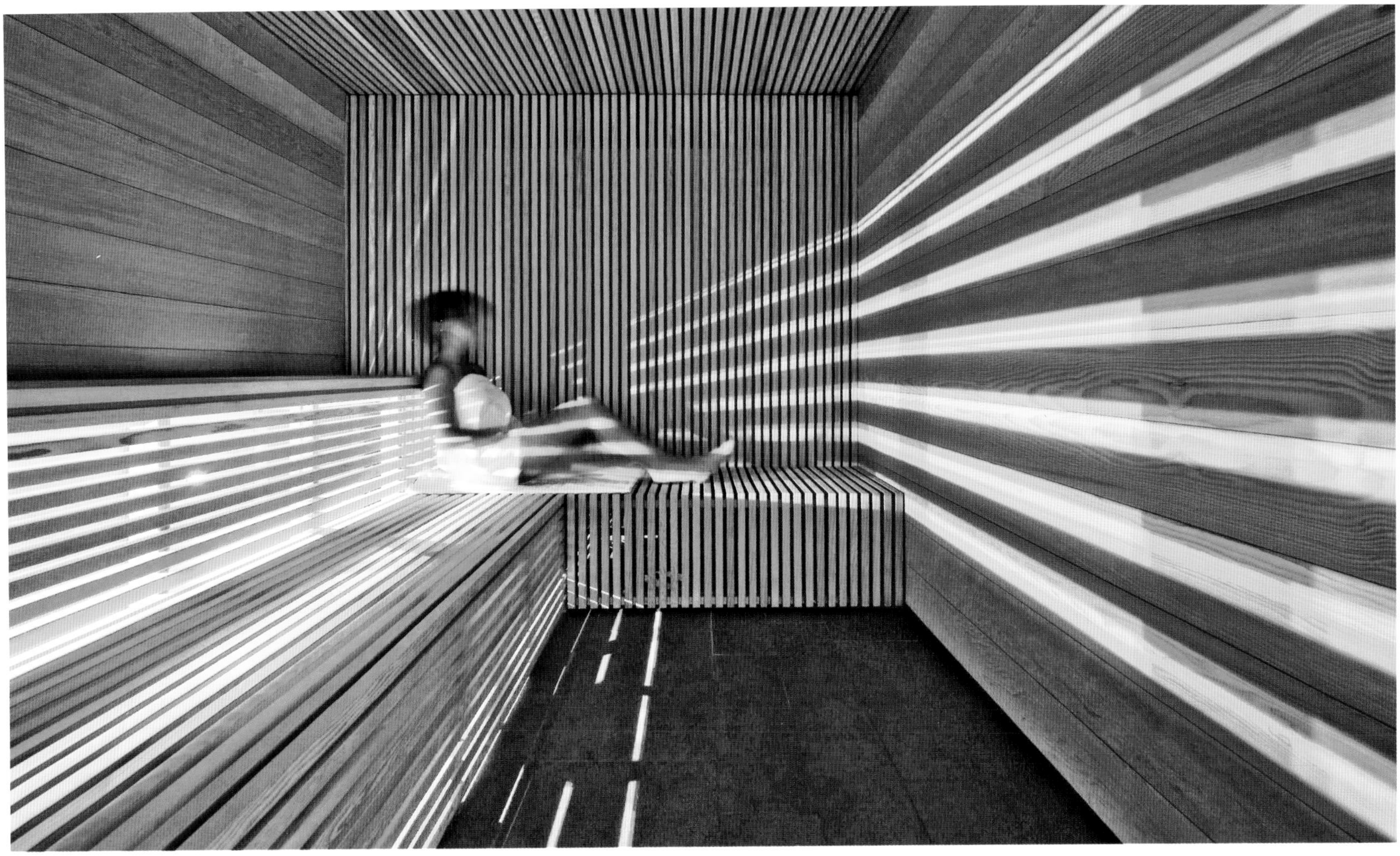

Parco Acque ai Cappuccini

Simone Micheli

Client: Park Hotel ai Cappuccini
Location: Park Hotel ai Cappuccini, Gubbio (PG), Italy
Area: 3,000 m^2
Photography: Juergen Eheim
Year: 2012

The "Parco Acque" is the new wellness center that "Park Hotel ai Cappuccini" reserves to his guests from last spring.

We can define Simone Micheli's work as an introspective journey whose destination is "relax". Let be together harmo-niously an ancient structure matrix (a seventeenth century monastery) with future design and technology: a challenge that Architect Micheli has won working on the concept of wonder.

The project is a dense connection of stories and truths, from the past to the future, imbued with the history and with the genius of a timeless place as Gubbio are. The main area of the wellness center is the pools zone where Simone Micheli says "the fluid and multiform matrix of the water is wonderfully exalted by bright, fun and interactive interior design"

A playful, dreamy and enterprising mood is the result of an amount of different elements such as: the stranding mesh holding in the air a gigantic jellow ball, a "curl-fountain" faucet and a rounded boardwalk in order to separate the swimming area from the first whirlpool zone.

Aetherea Concept Spa

Studio Bizzarro & Partners

Location: Milan
Photography: Luca Casonato

A small, intimate, wonderful microcosm. It's the place to get lost in the embrace of the senses, dreaming of being elsewhere, floating in the air and in contact with nothing but your own senses.

A carpet of dark earth to walk on barefoot, the enveloping wooden surface that embraces and encompasses small corners of peace and relaxation:

- The depth of water that gushes from the earth;

- The energy generated by a cool shower like a storm in the forest;

- The warmth of a finnish sauna;

- The ray of light descending from above, from the branches, looking like a cloud of gravity;

- The flickering fire flame that tries to climb up;

- The protection of a cave to get lost in a steam bath;

- A soft alcove suspended like a hammock between the trees.

This is an ethereal image of a wellness suite, lost in nature. A haven of peace, in an immaterial dimension that unveils the most primitive needs, which is imbued with the feeling of being suspended in space and time.

Angsana Spa Seaview Xiamen

Angsana Spa

Location: Xiamen, China

Angsana Spa, the award-winning sister brand of the renowned Banyan Tree Spa, debuts in Xiamen with the opening of Angsana Spa Seaview Xiamen. Being the first international spa to extend its foray in this flourishing city on the southeast coast of China, Angsana Spa greets spa aficionados with a refreshing blend of treatments and fusion of techniques from the East and West.

Xiamen boasts lush natural scenery with azure seas. Nestled on the picturesque beach line of the city, Seaview Resort Xiamen sits at a mountain foot and faces the sea. It features 500,000 square metres of evergreen gardens with luxurious accommodation. Angsana Spa is poised to become a tranquil haven which complements the tropical holiday experience.

Banyan Tree Spa Shanghai On The Bund

Banyan Tree Spa

Location: Shanghai, China

Banyan Tree Spa brings its award-winning blend of Asian therapies to greater heights with the launch of the Spa at Banyan Tree Shanghai On The Bund, Shanghai's first all river view hotel. This marks the second outlet in Shanghai following Banyan Tree Spa's debut in the city in 2003 and the group's seventh spa in Greater China. Discover a sensory experience at Banyan Tree Spa.

Located in Shanghai's iconic Bund district, the Spa is close to both historic landmarks and the new cultural and commercial centres of the cosmopolitan city. Spanning over 1,300 square metres over three floors within the urban resort, the award-winning spa features 11 exquisitely appointed treatment rooms including two Imperial Rooms with a Rainmist facility or Thai Massage area, four Double Deluxe Rooms and five Single Rooms. The name of each room is inspired by the 24 Chinese solar terms. For a rejuvenating wellness experience, the spa is complemented by a beauty salon, nail bar and Banyan Tree Gallery.

Embracing the local culture and traditional Chinese healing philosophy, Banyan Tree Spa Shanghai On the Bund's design concept is themed on the Five Elements, which are translated into unique colours and inspirations.

The Spa showcases a contemporary design combining sleek lines with traditional materials. Warm lighting, an inviting reception area which exudes elegance with a clear glass panel embedded with grey criss-cross textured patterns, a beige sofa and silk floral-motif throw cushions are just a few of the comforting touches.

A Spa stairway leads down to treatment rooms with sunlight streaming in from a skylight overhead. The walkway of treatment rooms is framed on one side by a two-storey wall of vivid green plants which embraces nature, with a contrasting dark wooden wall opposite which features symmetrical vertical metallic strips.

Treatment rooms draw reference from the Five Elements of gold, wood, water, fire and earth in their design. The Water-themed rooms feature clean horizontal lines across the ceiling and crystal-blue lighting; Gold-themed rooms include classic matte gold accents; Fire-themed rooms showcase vibrant red hues; and Wood and Earth rooms feature soothing neutral tones.

BANYAN TREE
GALLERY

Spa "Amore e Psiche" – Hotel Chateau Monfort

FZI Interiors

Location: Milano
Client: Planetaria Hotels
Photography: Stefano Oppo

In the dungeons of Chateau Monfort, a five stars hotel in the centre of Milan, Fzi Interiors created an original spa dedicated to the mythological gods Amore and Psyche. The ambience is relaxing and evocative, in line with the concept of the building. The dream of the urban castle continues in its basement, where there's a hidden and magic world, far from the stressful rhythm of the city. Behind glass doors, the natural marble pavements match with the coarse texture of the bronze walls like desert sand. The circle downpour of the agora falls on little stones, giving energy to the room and reflecting the soft lightning outwards.

Three synchronized jets of water come out of the wall, sided by the Mediterranean bath and a wooden sauna.

A corridor leads to a wide room with a hot bench that looks towards a salty pool: enlightened from the inside and dominated by an eccentric iron chandelier, the water stays still, crystallized and surrounded by silence.

Separated by a glass at the other side of the pool, a relaxing area is glamorized by little details and bag chairs in a beige tissue, which give an exotic touch to the ambience.

The changing rooms are linked to a common space with a long round mirror and heavy curtains. The spa continues with the treatment rooms, one for massages and mud baths, with a stone couch topped by a shower jet, another one with a round floating bath of salty water. A private spa is also hidden behind a secret door in a bookshelf outside the wellness area. Inside, low lights, silence and a sexy atmosphere surrounds the bath, the relaxing chair, and the hot rooms. Everything is exclusive, warm and smooth, like it is in the best fantastic dreams.

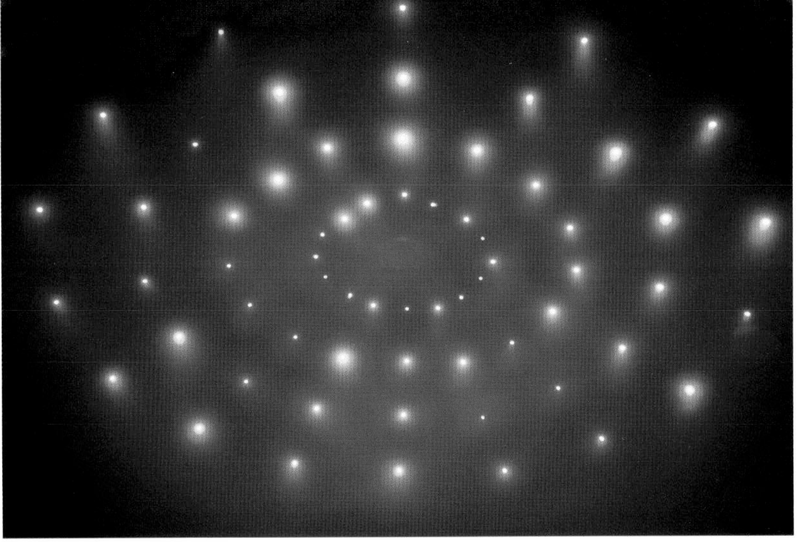

UNIVERSITY COLLEGE
BIRMINGHAM

Spa "Le Terme di Kyoto" – Enterprise Hotel

FZI Interiors

Location: Milano
Client: Planetaria Hotels
Photography: Stefano Oppo

Situated at the seventh floor of the Enterprise Hotel, with a panoramic view on Milan, Terme di Kyoto is an exclusive wellness area that melts Japanese style and glamour. Tissues and colours are chosen in line with the concept of the modern and classy four star hotel. Open spaces, glass séparés with white flower applications, minimal shelves in dark wood, give to the spa a strong oriental touch. Everything is composed in detail, from the square pool to the hot bench in white-mosaic, from the soft lamps to the tatami, from the little candles here and there, to the original gong, standing at one side of the room. The relaxing area is created as a real bedroom, with two beds in Japanese style, surrounded by warm wood and decorated with nature inspired drawings at the walls. The ambience is perfect to let skilful hands help bodies to relax with shiatzu, thai and ayurvedic massages. Precious materials and clean shapes are also used in the sauna, in the steam bath and in the simple changing rooms. A large window lets the natural light come in the main room, and also gives a wonderful view on the roofs of Milan, which becomes magic in the dark. According with the light, the setting is simpler and more traditional during the day, while it looks smarter and more exclusive at night: what never change, are silence, privacy and wellness.

RGB

京の湯

ESPA Spa at ICC Ritz Carlton

HBA

Design: Team led by Inge Moore, President Europe HBA
Location: Hong Kong
Photography: HBA

The Ritz-Carlton ESPA: Cocooned among the Clouds: In the 21st century, with easy international mobility and more frequent and opulent luxury travel, the spa-goer is increasingly demanding of the spa experience. All spas have the functional goal of being a place to leave the cares and concerns of a busy world behind, so there is certain expectation of sameness within the realm of the urban spa. The nearly 10,000 square foot Ritz-Carlton spa by ESPA floats those expectations away from the mind at the moment of entry. Stepping into the spa's reception area is moving from one state to another. More than 1,000 feet above the frenetic streets of Hong Kong, the guest is simultaneously attached to the city with breathtaking views in clear days, yet insulated from it.

Using "cocooned among the clouds" as a governing narrative, HBA planned spaces without any sharp corners. All edges are rounded, and the walls themselves are curved as if in a protective embrace.

ESPA

Entre Cielos Hotel & Spa

A4estudio

Architects: Leonardo Codina, Juan Manuel Filice
Location: Luján de Cuyo, Mendoza, Argentina
Area: 597 m^2

Rest and relaxation were the main objectives of this assignment. Its location on the outskirts of the city of Mendoza and its natural environment of vineyards, fruit trees, poplars and views of the Andes were part of this tapestry of Mendoza where we will develop the tourism complex.

In a land of an old vineyard of 100 meters of frontage and 400 in length, the project is structured from a pedestrian path that connects its buildings in an east-west orientation. This situation forces the visitors to leave their vehicle at the access parking lot to enter the campus on foot, as an act of neglect and separation from the outside.

A series of outdoor spaces that occur along this path will be discovered and lived in a playful experience that attempts to arouse the visitor's sensitive attitudes and to predispose them to experience powerfully the complex.

At the Spa, the space is defined totally isolated from the outside. Elements that define the space are located with the intention of creating a course of baths, steam and massage rooms, add a perimeter wall that encloses it, deprives it of its visual relationship with the outside world and turns it into a space that arises from light. So small openings in walls and ceilings create backlight, details, and rates qualifying spaces and motivate senses.

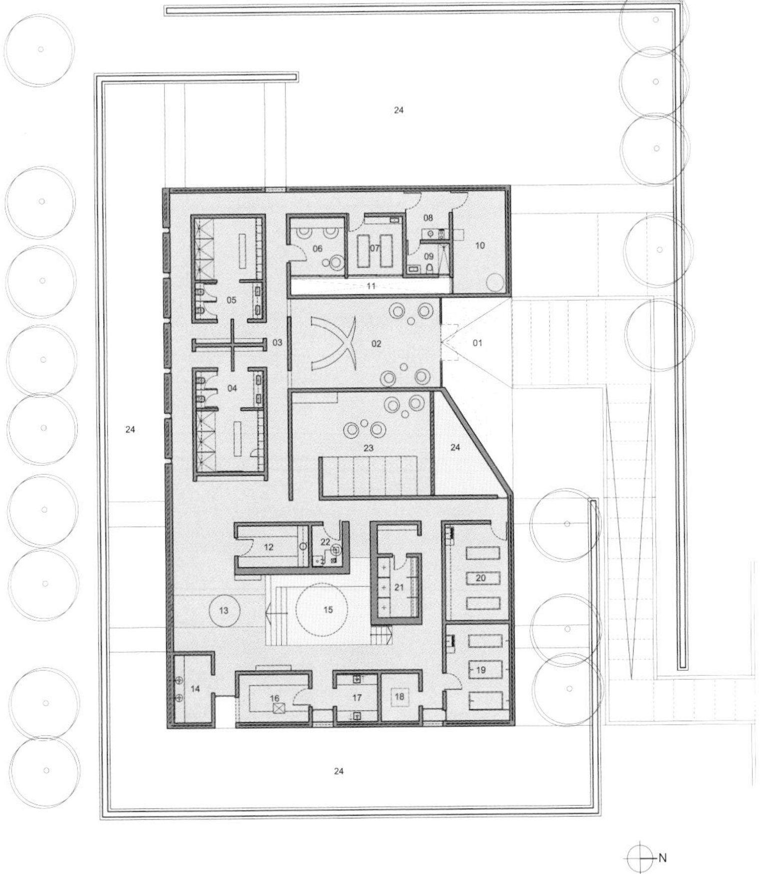
24
06
07
08
09
10
11
05
03
02
01
04
24
23
24
12
22
21
20
13
15
19
14
16
17
18
24
N
PLANTA

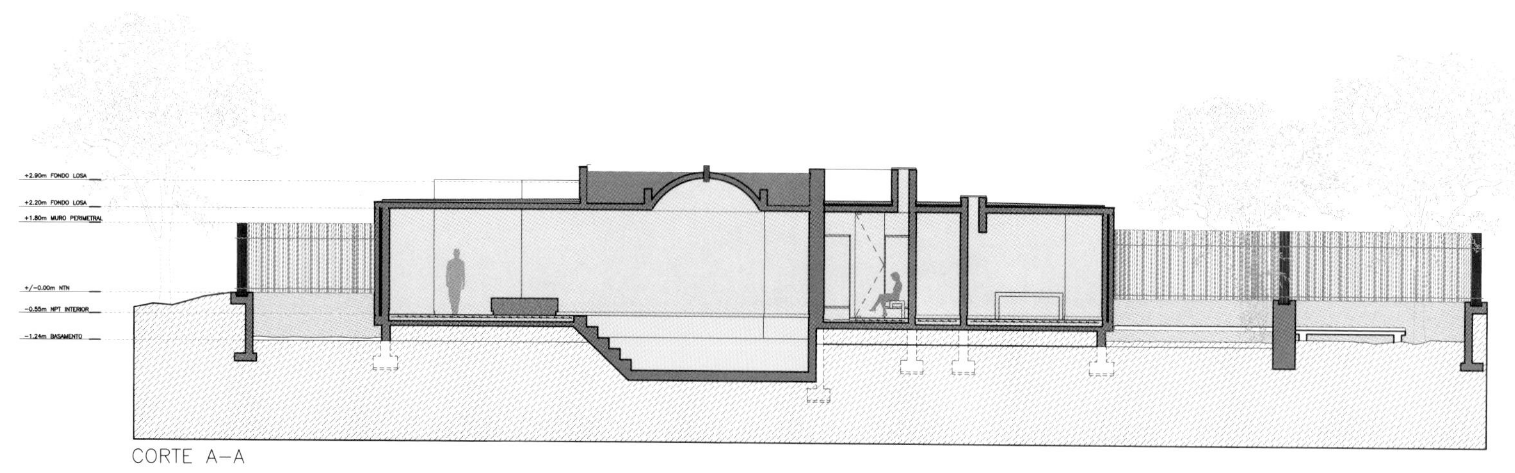
+2.90m FONDO LOSA
+2.20m FONDO LOSA
+1.80m MURO PERIMETRAL
+/-0.00m NTN
-0.55m NPT INTERIOR
-1.24m BASAMENTO

CORTE A–A

Wellness Centre Termalija

Enota

Project Team: Dean Lah, Milan Tomac, Anže Zalaznik, Petra Ostanek, Tinka Prekovič, Grega Tramte
Client: Terme Olimia
Location: Podčetrtek, Slovenia
Area: 7,140 m^2
Photograpgher: Miran Kambič

Wellness Centre Termalija is designed as an extension of the existing spa at Terme Olimia in Podčetrtek. Growth of the accommodation capacities of the thermal complex has led to the need to increase the space around the spa's pool area. At the same time, the investor wanted to build a new modern sauna center and before all establish a covered link between closed and opened parts of the spa, which is also covered during the winter.

Space intended for extension was very limited. Any intervention in the pool area would immensely impair the quality of space in the summer, when it is very important that the pools have many well-regulated open areas. Therefore, we found room for expansion in a narrow zone alongside the access road which winds around the existing building. New building is distinctively separated from the old one and is somehow embracing it. From the access road side it is forming a completely new facade of the spa while seen from the inside of the thermal complex it is almost invisible and does not alter the character of space.

Extension of the Wellness Centre Termalija is designed as a sequence of different theme areas that address visitors through their own experience gained from the world of nature. Animation of numerous visitors' senses in creating a unique experience was a guideline for designing the spaces. Spaces are of different colors and decorated with stylized graphic drawings derived from nature (vision), ambience music and tones taken from the nature differ from space to space (hearing) and the ventilation system is additionally equipped with a system that emanates aroma, which also alters from space to space (smell).

Since the building, due to its size, significantly stands out in the surrounding, predominantly rural architecture, it is designed in a very reserved manner. The building appears almost as a fence that protects the spa complex space from a gaze from the road in front of it. Although the new facility occupies an area adjacent to the road and does not take any quality space from the pool area, the roof is planted with greenery and is available for public access. In this way, the newly acquired area compensates a part of the ground terrain that was taken away and offers completely new and different experience of the space. The green roof is folded and it seems to, due to the fusion of the planted areas, naturally continue into the surrounding landscape.

If the building functions reserved during the day, it shows a completely different face at night when the rural environment is no longer present. Illuminated interior then flares up in all the "colors of nature." Due to its colorful interior, the facility looks as 'a billboard'. A billboard that invites passers-by to step inside and to the guests of the spa complex indicates the target of their trip.

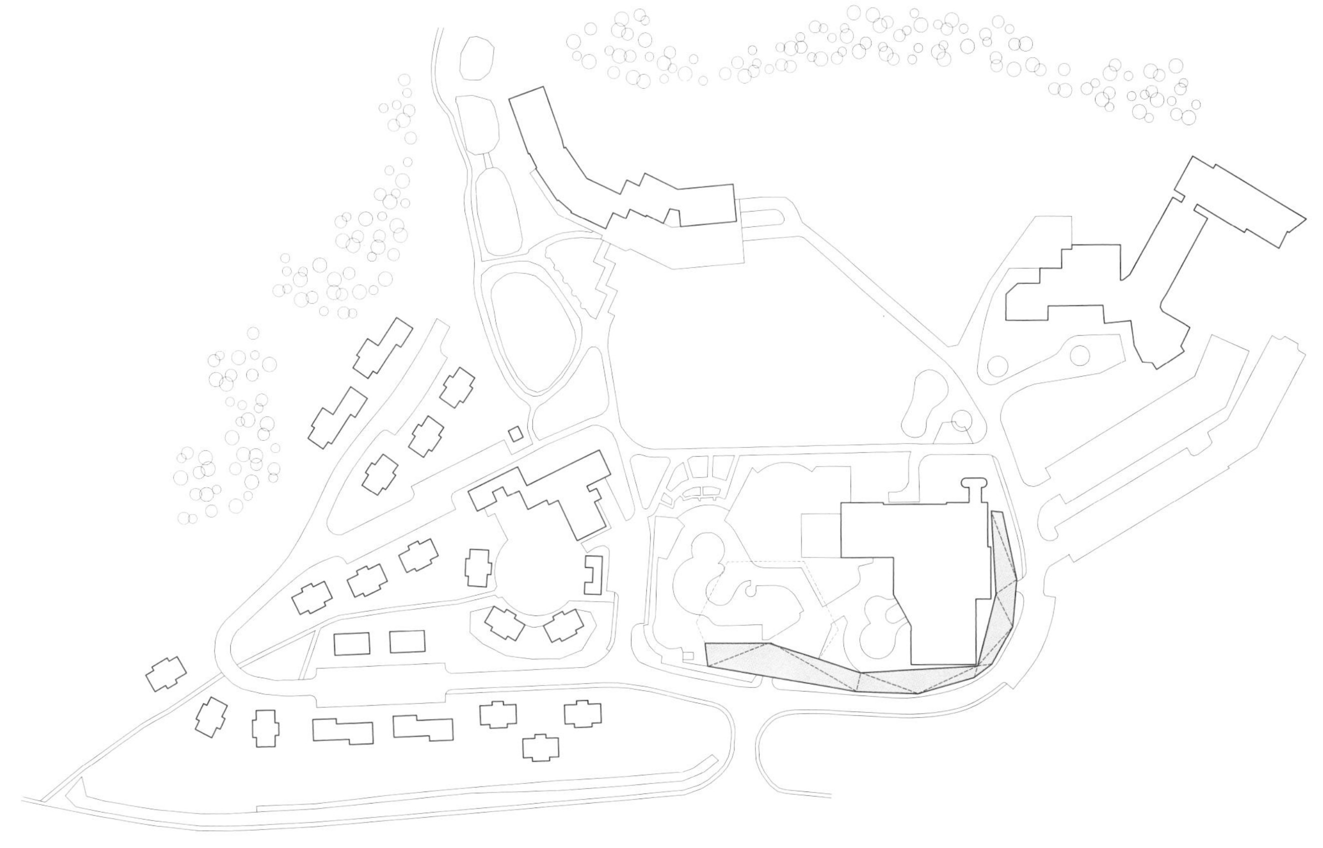

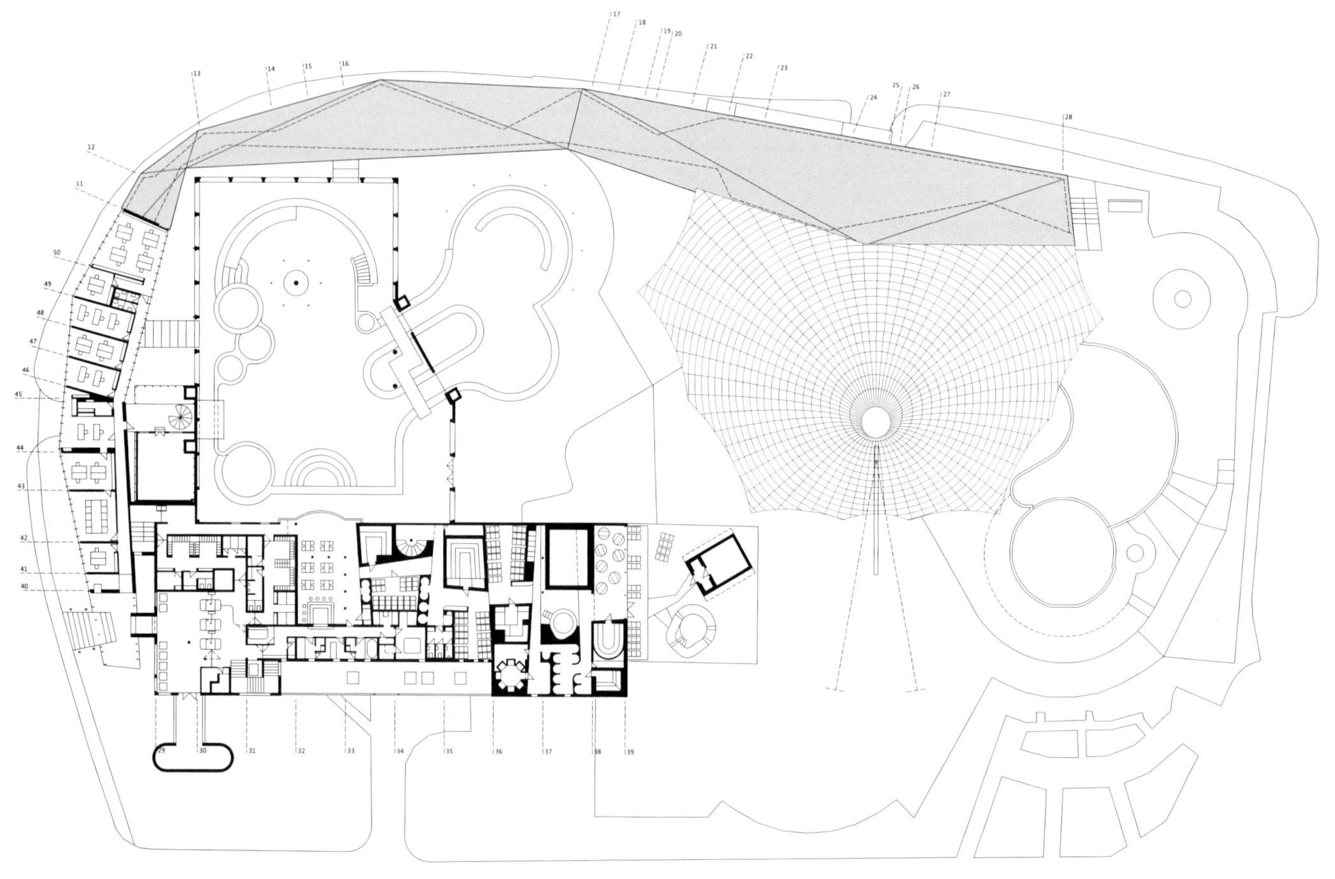

02 termalija first floor plan (1-600)

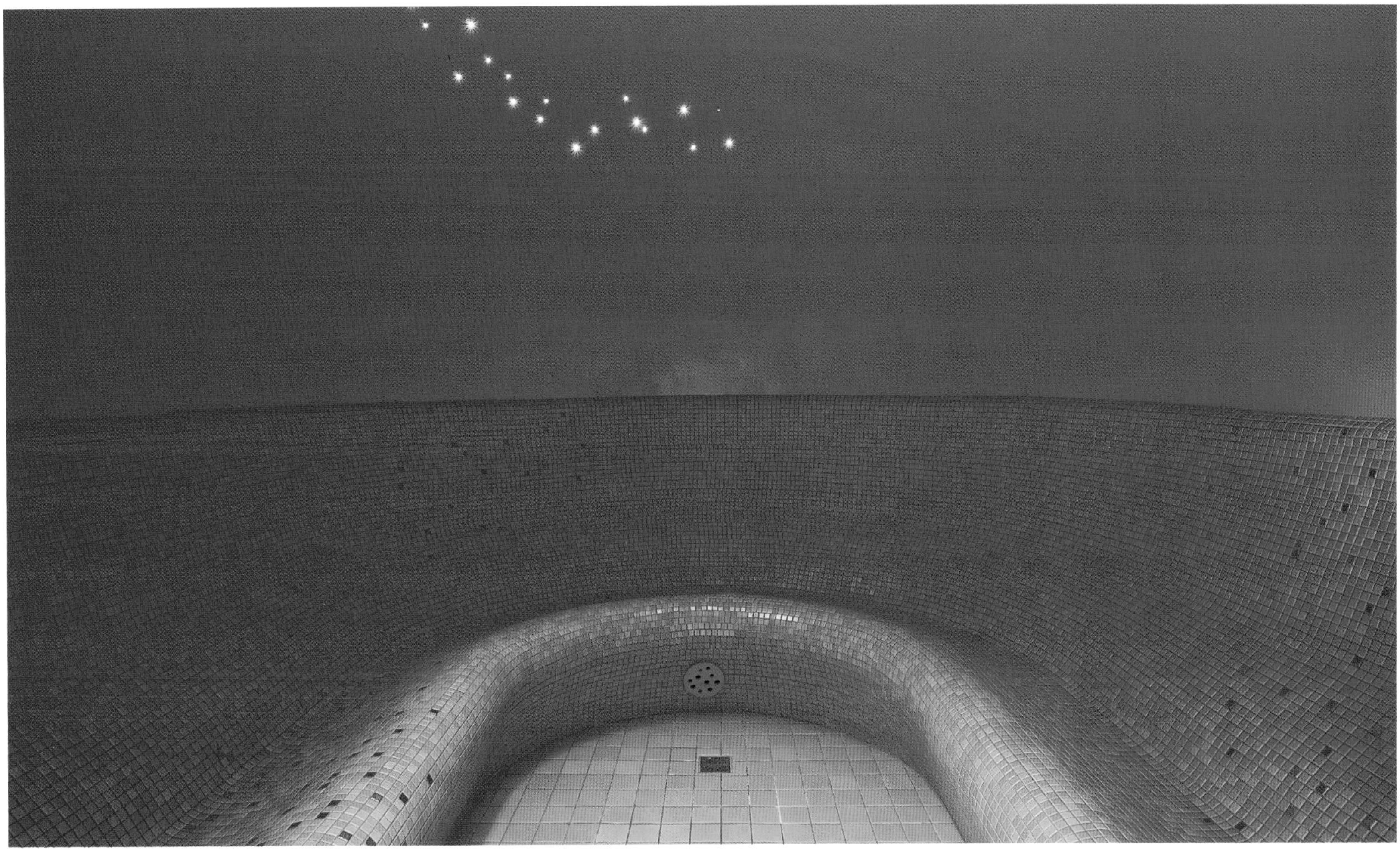

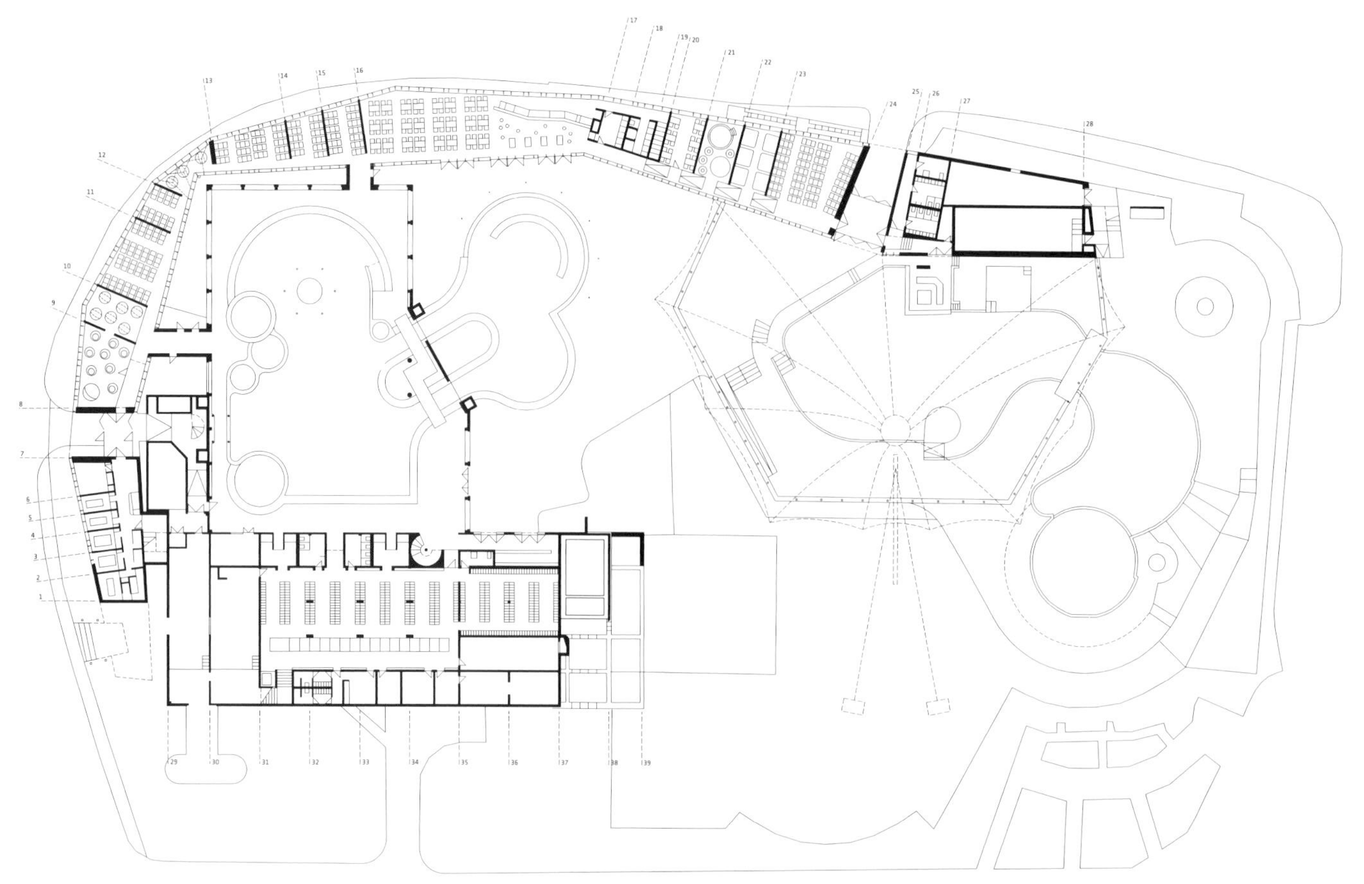

01 termalija ground floor plan (1-600)

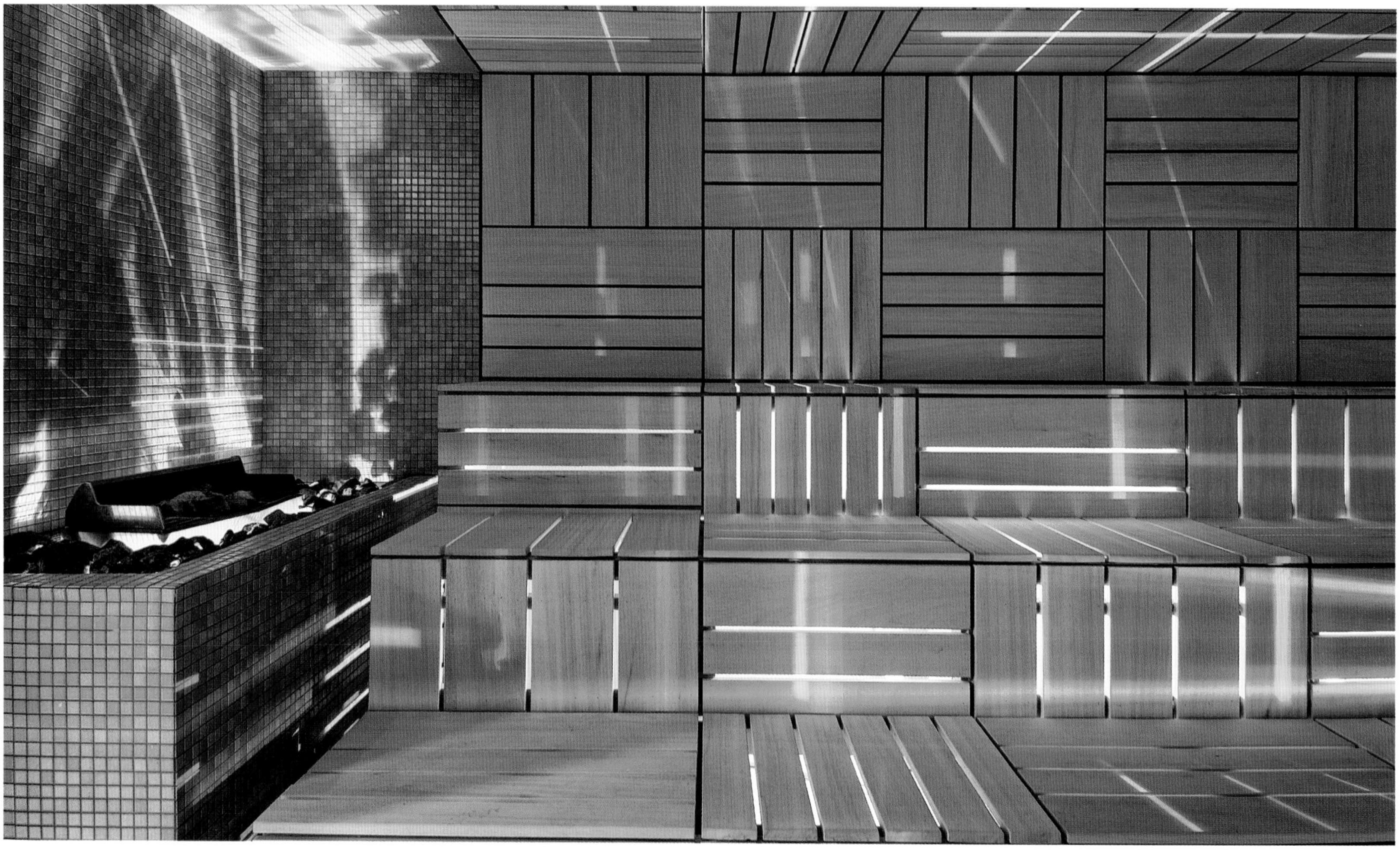

Borgo Brufa Spa Resort

Silvia Giannini Architetto

Client: Borgo Brufa S.n.c di Andrea Sfascia & C.
Location: Brufa di Torgiano (PG), Italy
Photography: Pier Paolo Metelli

The project of Borgo Brufa Spa Resort originates from the will to link the Spa to the structure and to the surroundings.

The Resort is a structure of detached type, consisting of stone houses, among the green of aromatic plants, olive trees and bushes, in an area with an open sight on the Assisi hills, and the Spa relates with materials and colours of the landscape.

The intervention was both of complete restructuring of wellness centre spaces and of expansion to a total area of 1400 square meters, to make the SPA the attraction centre in the structure: the characterizing element is the indoor/outdoor swimming pool heated and equipped with ornamental waterworks, while the sight ranges over the hills as far as the eye can see.

The rooms for massages open on a curved wooden passage ; inside these rooms have different chromatisms, all coming from indirect lights hidden by a wooden strip.

The damp area is imagined like a street inside the village ("borgo"): the stone wall, the olive tree in the middle of a large flower bed, the fountain in cobblestones; the floor itself is made of pebbles.

Walking in this resort, you will discover the various attractions, as entering small squares: emotional showers, Turkish bath, sauna, vitalizing showers, fountain of ice. At the end of the course there is the stars room: a room for relaxation, characterized by optical fibres on the ceiling, walls and floor. Another particular element of the damp area is the saline grotto: a pond of floating enriched with mineral salts and underwater lighting that changes colours and reflects this chromatism all around the interior and on the white iridescent mosaics.

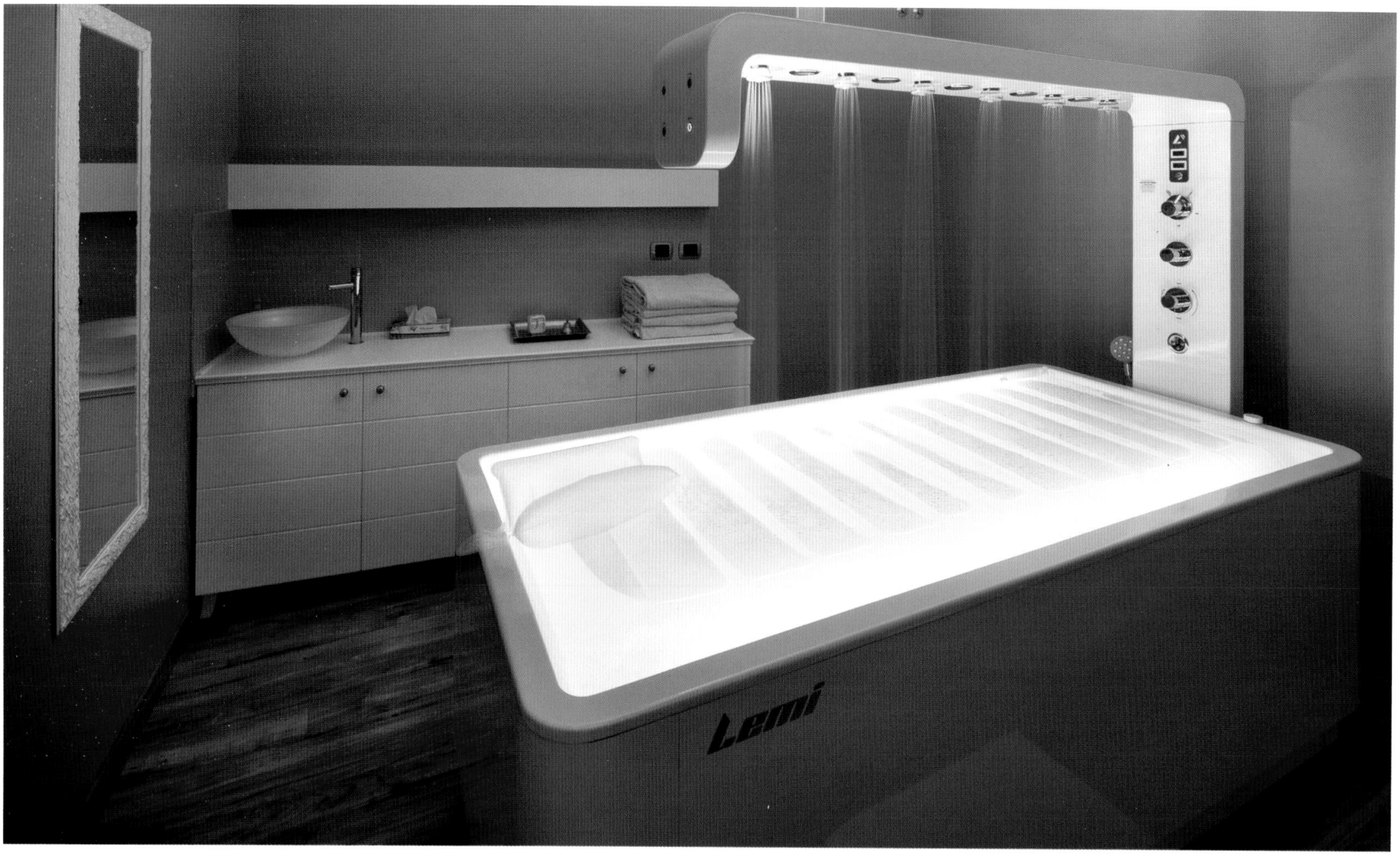

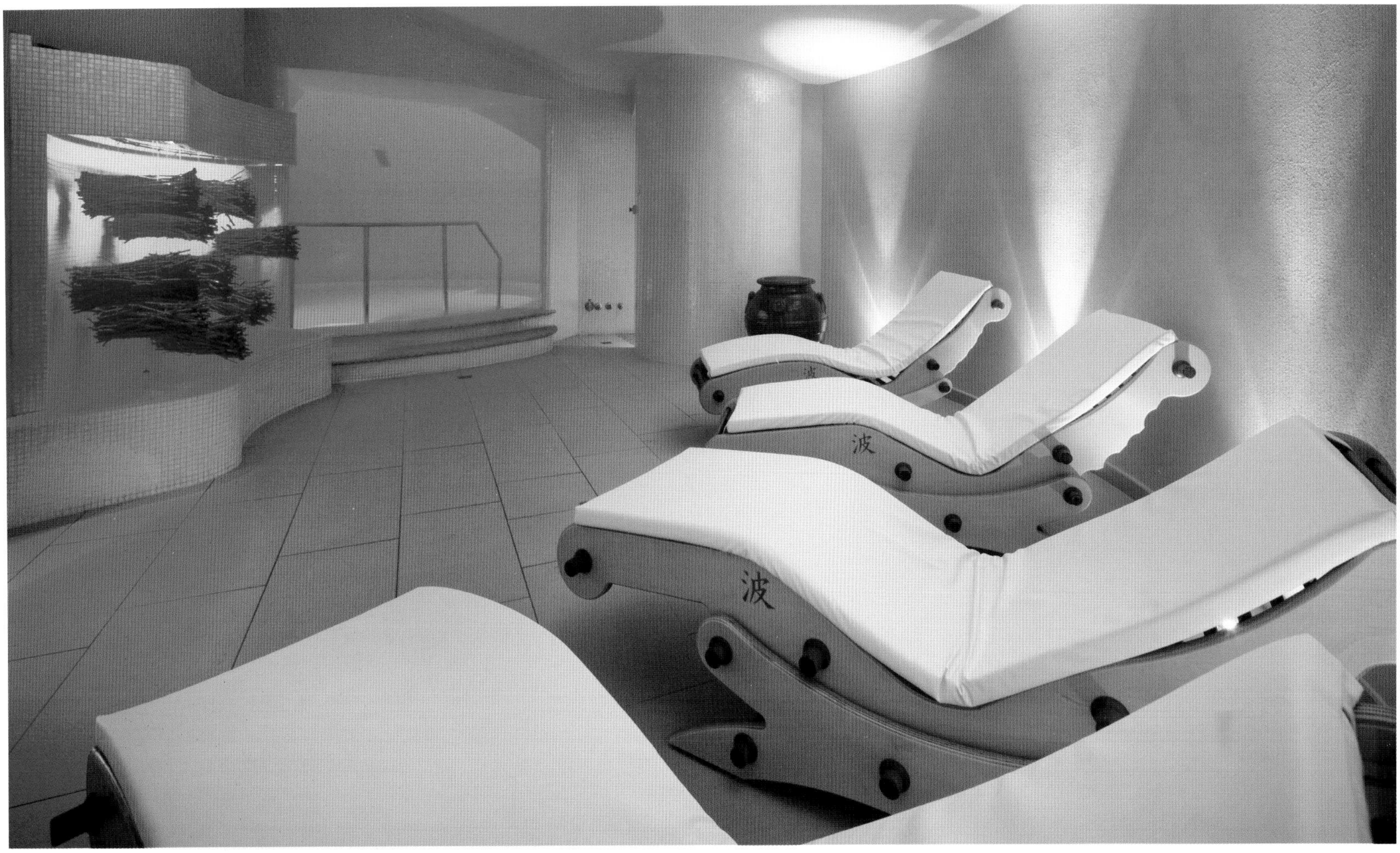

ESPA Spa at the Istanbul Edition Hotel

HBA

HBA / Hirsch Bedner Associates, the leading global hospitality design firm of the world's most anticipated hotels, resorts and spas, has completed the design of the ESPA located in the groundbreaking Istanbul EDITION hotel. The Istanbul EDITION strives to provide guests with unique experiences and has allowed The Gallery, HBA's London studio to be creative and expressive with their design resulting in a memorable and incomparable space.

With the ESPA, HBA London designed a contemporary, state-of-the-art spa with design influences drawn from Turkish tradition and local customs. The indulgent and breathtaking spa incorporates beauty, health and wellness that are both social and the ultimate in luxury.

Spread over three floors, this extraordinary 20,000 square foot spa is truly spectacular with dark and sumptuous lighting, rich metallic woods, embossed bronze floors, sumptuous seating and walls upholstered in exquisite horsehair. Crystals are also delicately integrated into the spa design. The combination of these unique design elements help to create the perfect space to lose oneself and forget the stresses and strains of the outside world.

According to Nathan Hutchins, Associate HBA London, "The ESPA at the Istanbul Edition journey is one of comfort, glamour and alluring charm featuring mysterious spaces to relax and rejuvenate. Inspiration for the spa's design was taken from the faceted cut out patterns found in a traditional Hammam to create a subtle yet atmospheric feeling using light and dark."

"The play of light was the other main component in the design inspiration, creating shadows and shafts of light in unexpected spaces," says Inge Moore, Principal. "These concepts married with a rich selection of materials and rich wall paneling creates luxurious,

alluring, opulent spaces that make the guest feel both indulged and protected...our aim was to design a spa that creates an unforgettable experience."

The Hammam, a truly focal and grand tradition to a Turkish Spa becomes an intimate and exclusive haven at the ESPA. Opulent chocolate brown marble and cast bronze sinks create a deep sense of calm and warmth throughout the Hammam, with scrub and steam rooms to soothe the mind and cleanse the body.

A comprehensive menu of beauty and health treatments is offered in the multiple treatment rooms, which include a VIP suite decorated with patterned leather floors and smoked onyx walls where couples can unwind in the oversize bathtub, steam shower and unique relaxation bed suspended from the ceiling. A stunning pool and a state-of-the-art fitness center complete this extraordinary experience.

Dhara Wellness

Studio Alberto Apostoli

Client: Consolini Hotels
Location: Brenzone, Verona, Italy
Photography: Maurizio Marcato

In Brenzone, on the Venetian side of Lake Garda, the Consolini Group decided to give the Belfiore Park Hotel a decidedly ayurvedic dimension by opening a new wellness centre spread along an entire floor of the hotel and named the Dhara Wellness. The project aimed to create a balance between the classical elements of the SPA by carefully studying spaces, forms, materials, colours and lights. The architect Alberto Apostoli, responsible of the project, commented: "The space is very homogeneous from an aesthetic point of view but it is also full of innovative solutions, and small details that were constructed with. I care and respect for the territory combined with a new cultural approach". By taking advantage of the local materials, the particularities of the location and a natural spring that was discovered during the construction, the SPA obtains a sensorial environment that is alive with every construction detail and material that was specially designed for it. Following a characteristic horizontal element made with bamboo canes that run along the entire floor leading to the SPA, one enters, or rather "filters in", a socializing room that is neutral and contemporary.

A final element is the large olive tree that was placed within the structure during the intervention; it was originally from the land adjacent to the Hotel. The geometrical and emotional core of the SPA is a basin of water that is constantly replenished by the natural spring whose waters are utilized almost as a lining as it flows directly onto the bare stone. Within the basin, there is a shower that is made by a particular element that is the local stone and a special Kneipp treatment composed by single pools that are also made in the local stone. The sauna, another strong element of the centre, is created entirely in stone and is characterized by a large glass partition for the unusual transfer to the basin of water. Alongside the sauna is a vapour bath, covered by a special mosaic in resin whose parts "digitally" recreate the intertwined branches of the lemon trees. The relax area is positioned at the end of the centre and offers a magnificent view of the lake that is only a couple of meters away.

Ayurveda Rooms
Wellness
Meeting-Lounge

Armani/SPA

Armani Hotels & Resorts

Client: Armani Hotel Dubai
Location: Dubai, United Arab Emirates

An oasis of peace and tranquility in the heart of a bustling city, the 12,000 sqm Armani/SPA reflects the Armani lifestyle and design philosophy, offering unique spaces and outstanding service for individually personalised treatments, personal fitness, sequential thermal bathing, creative SPA cuisine or simply, private and social relaxation areas.

Each guest at the Armani/SPA receives a personal consultation from the spa professional to develop a bespoke sensory experience designed by Armani. The SPA therapies have been designed to fulfill different goals. MU quenches a desire for relaxation and stillness; Libert encourages freedom of movement and the release of physical pain; and Fluidit enhances vitality, restoring internal balance.

ARMANI / SPA

اكوا
Acqua
ساونا
Sauna

Thermal Baths Bad Ems

4a Architekten

Architects: Matthias Burkart, Alexander von Salmuth, Ernst Ulrich Tillmanns, Hallstrasse 25, D-70376 StuttgartClient: Emser Therme
Photography: David Matthiessen, Stuttgart

4a Architekten extend their bathing repertoire: The Bad Ems Thermal Baths proves itself with its distinct character and high standards of comfort

Since December 2012, the spa town of Bad Ems now has another new attraction: The new Bad Ems Thermal Baths designed by 4a Architekten is an architectural highlight that tempts visitors to the town and impresses its bathers with its high standards of comfort and its special atmosphere. The wellness bath is therefore a valuable addition to the wellness and recreational opportunities offered by the town, offering numerous factors and substantially strengthening the future position of Bad Ems in the health-cure and bathing landscape.

The changing-room and shower area is located on the ground floor together with the sauna. The changing rooms form a kind of lock gate between the publicly viewable connecting passage running along the north facade, and the showers that lead directly into the bathing hall. The largely transparent composition of the facade gives the hall a friendly atmosphere that is suffused with light. The free arrangement of the structures such as the steam bath and the pastille, the different pools and the distinctive design of the exposed concrete wall with its pebble-shaped sections provide a varied and lively appearance. The special ambience of well-being is created through the choice of friendly and cheerful colours, atmospheric lighting and perfectly matched materials: Anthracite-coloured porcelain stoneware, white-tiled pools with marble pool borders, ceiling panelling made from Aleppo pine, wall panelling made from Siberian larchwood slats, and brushed alder wood combine to give an impression of space. Visitors enter the sauna area through either the changing area or the bathing hall.

2.01 - Windfang
2.02 - Eingangshalle
2.03 - Shop/Boutique
2.04 - Kasse
2.05 - Bistro Eingang
2.06 - Küche
2.07 - Umkleiden
2.08 - Duschen/ WC Damen
2.09 - Duschen/WC Herren
2.10 - Behinderten WC
2.11 - Lager
2.12 - Badehalle
2.13 - Regenwolke
2.14 - Thermalbecken innen
2.15 - Warmsprudelbecken
2.16 - Restaurant Badehalle
2.17 - Schwimmmeister
2.18 - Sidroga Dampfbad
2.19 - Bewegungs- & Therapiebecken
2.20 - Kaltbecken
2.21 - Heißbecken
2.22 - Thermalaußenbecken
2.23 - Bewegungsbecken Sommer
2.24 - Saunabereich
2.25 - Tauchbecken
2.26 - Saunaraum
2.27 - Dampfbad
2.28 - Salzsauna
2.29 - Ruheraum
2.30 - Kaminzimmer
2.31 - Gartensauna

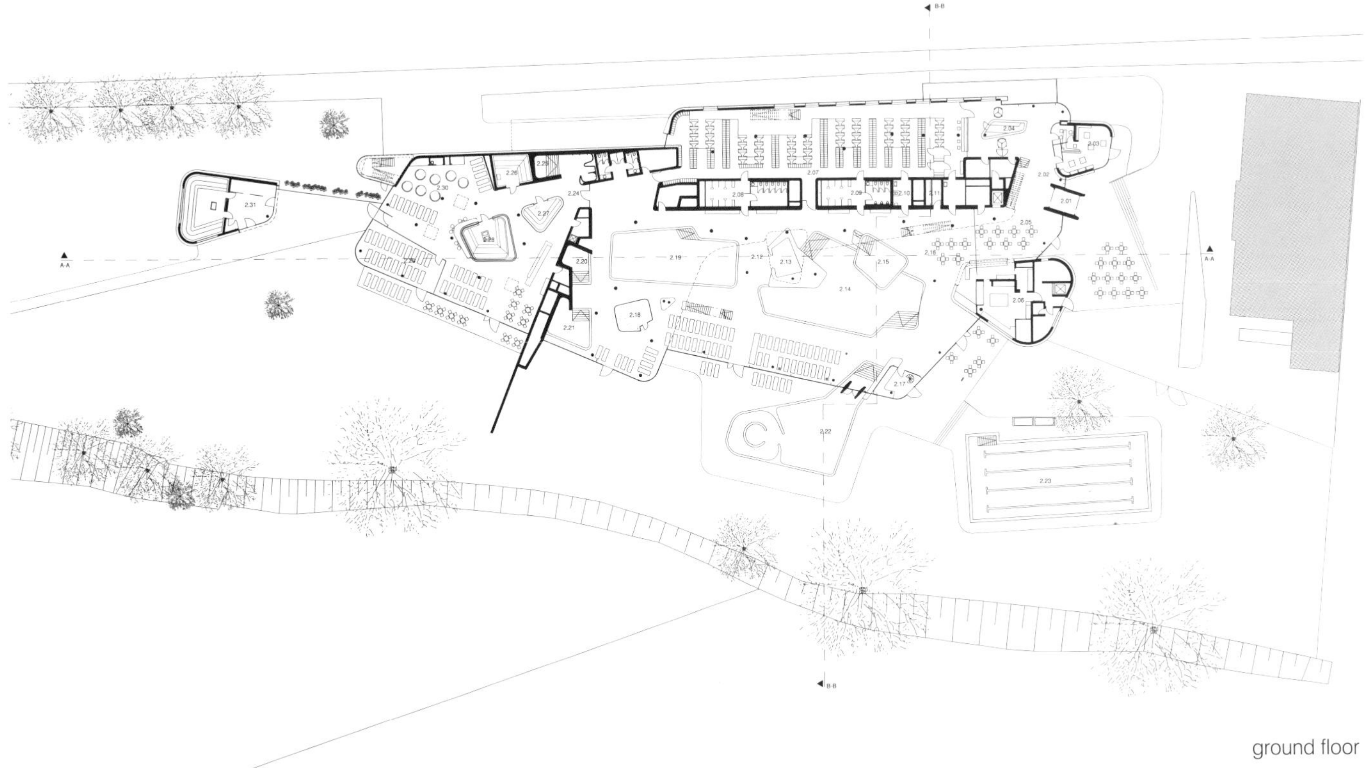

ground floor

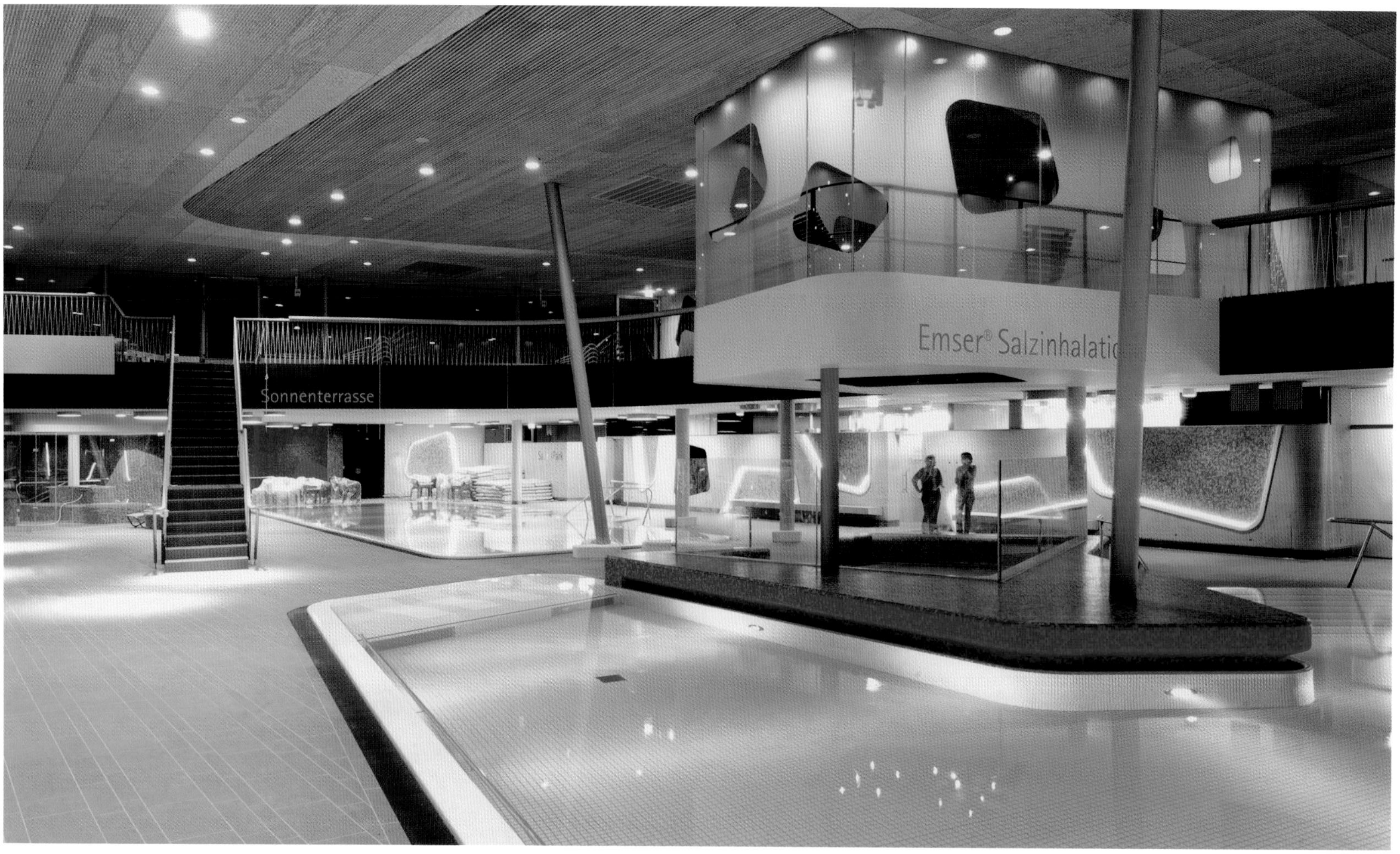

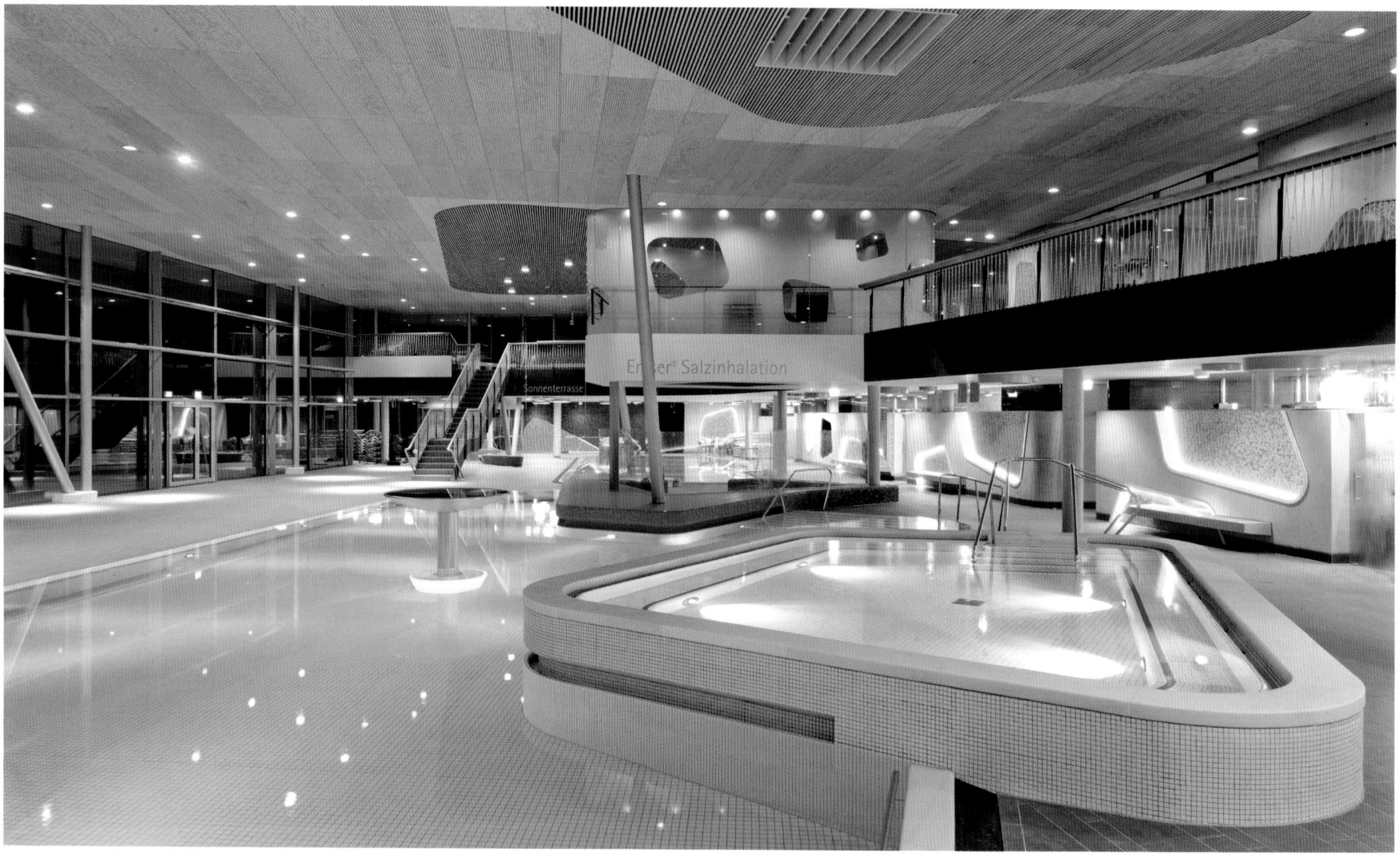

Restaurant

A circular route runs through the spacious single-level sauna landscape along the various sauna rooms, the open and enclosed relaxation areas and the sauna bar, finally leading to the spacious sauna garden where the Finnish sauna is located. Another highlight of the Bad Ems Thermal Baths is the river sauna which lies like a pebble in the River Lahn. This is due for completion in the summer of 2013. Guests can use a walkway to reach a platform with its own sauna facilities – two sauna rooms with a relaxation room and sauna bar. The secluded river sauna completes the diverse range of options available in the outdoor area and offers a space for rest and relaxation. During the summer months an outdoor exercise pool further enhances the range of bathing opportunities. The administration and staff rooms in the basement are similarly reached via a staircase in the lobby. The basement also accommodates the technical facilities for the entire building. Deliveries to the building arrive from the road via a ramp at the level of the sauna wing.

The new Bad Ems Thermal Baths is a successful example of how bathing culture and contemporary architecture can be combined by means of atmospheric design and high standards of comfort. After all, experience shows that bathers can only feel at ease, relax and find peace of mind in an atmosphere of the highest quality.

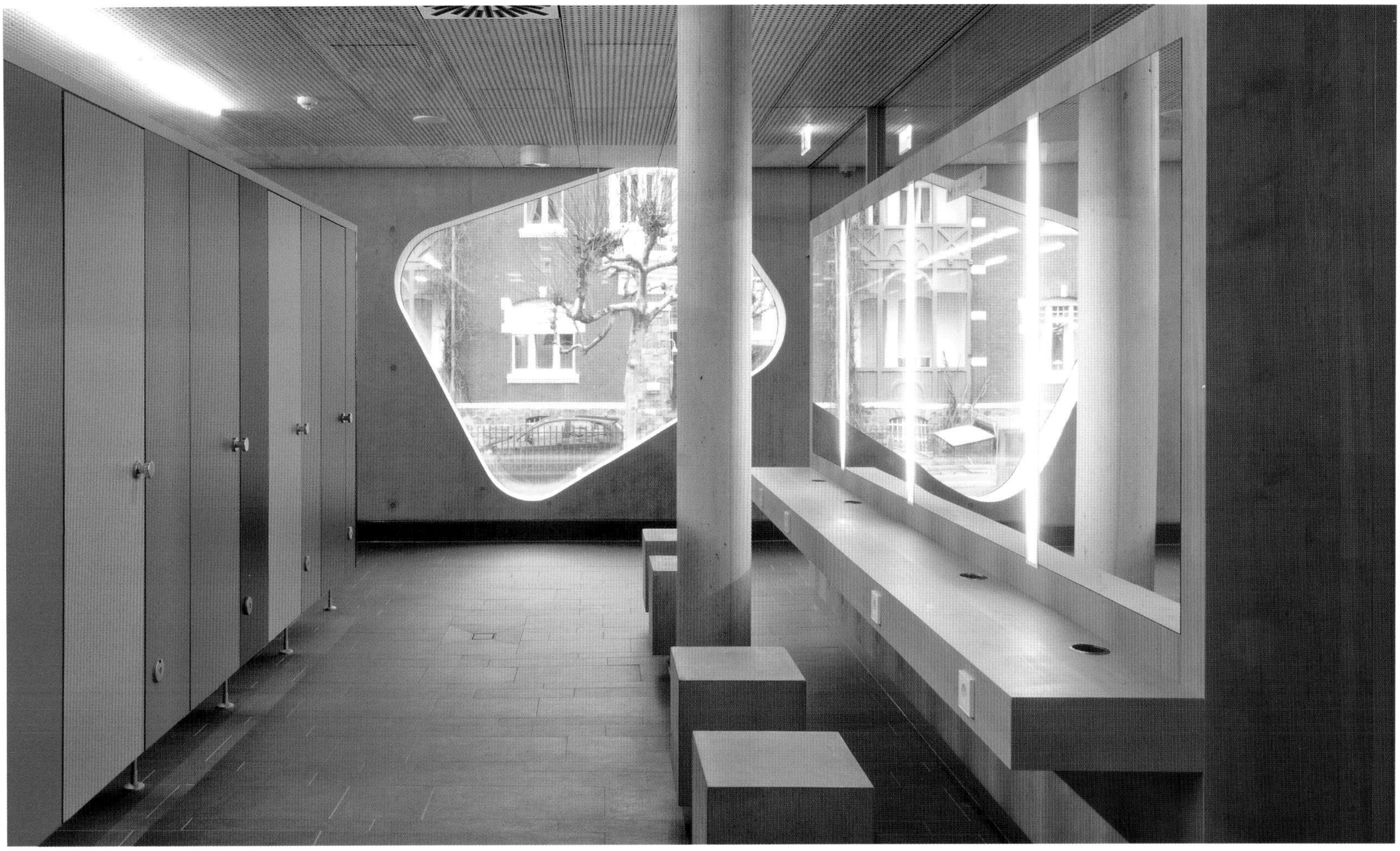

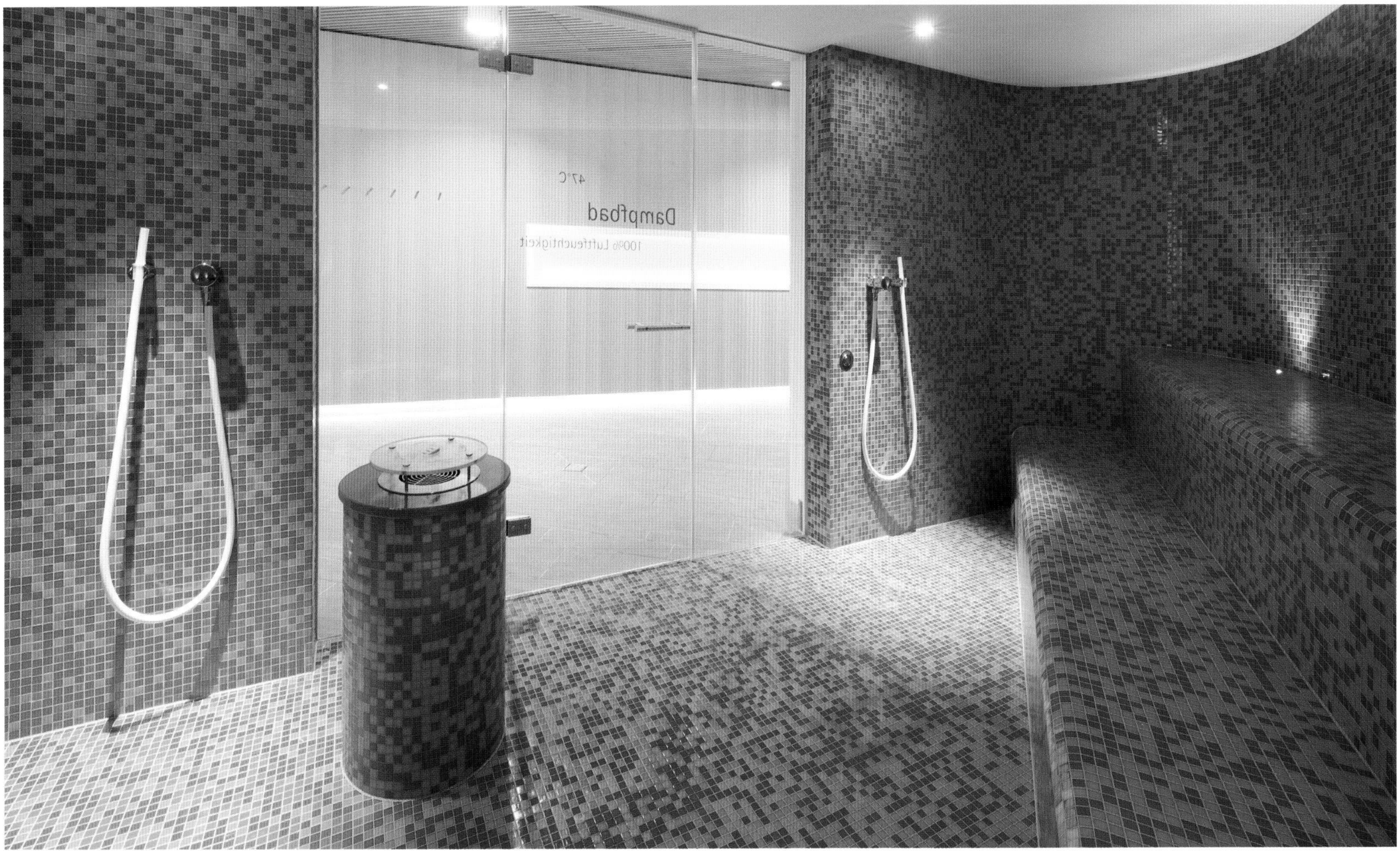
47°C
Dampfbad
100% Luftfeuchtigkeit

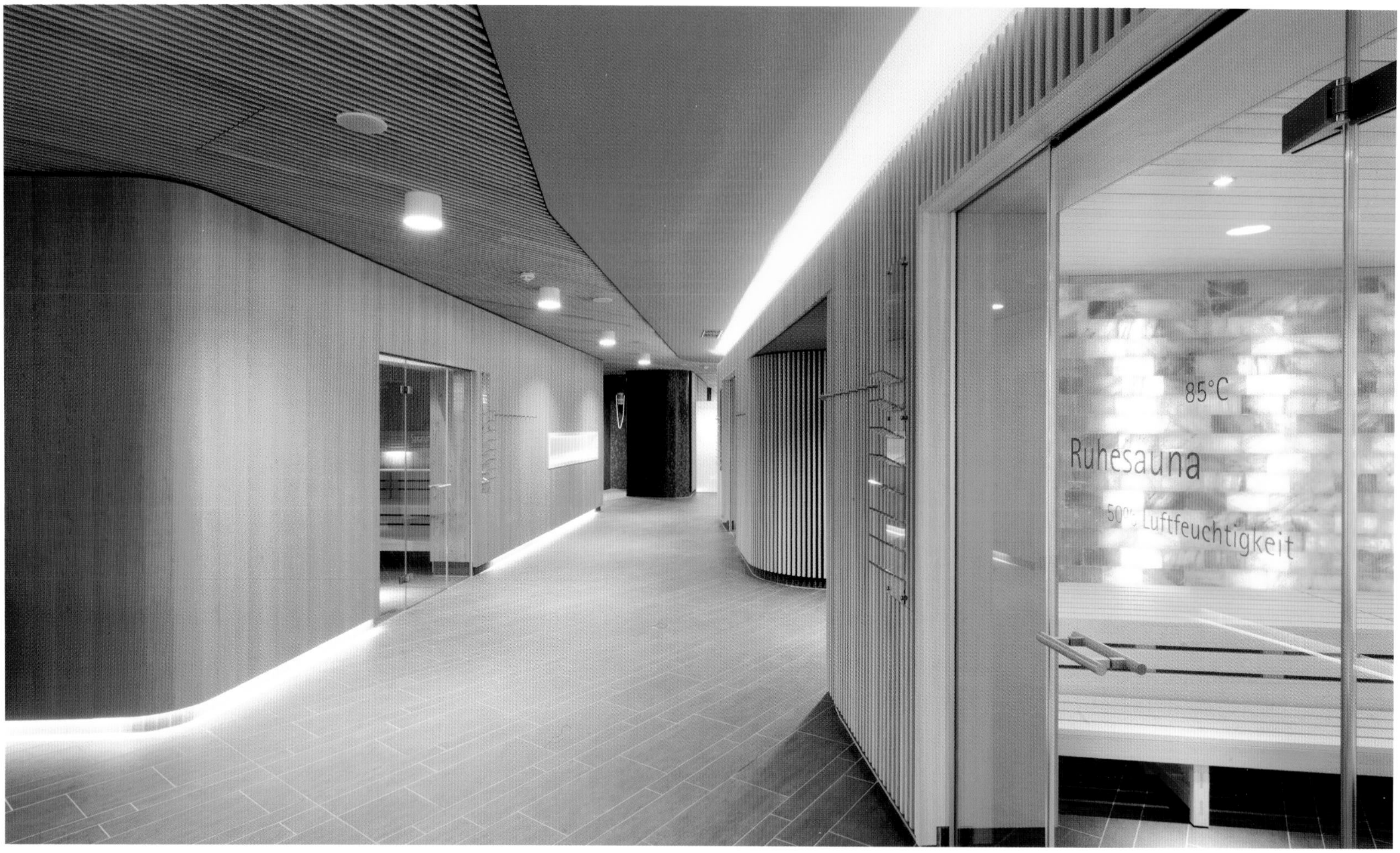
85°C
Ruhesauna
50% Luftfeuchtigkeit

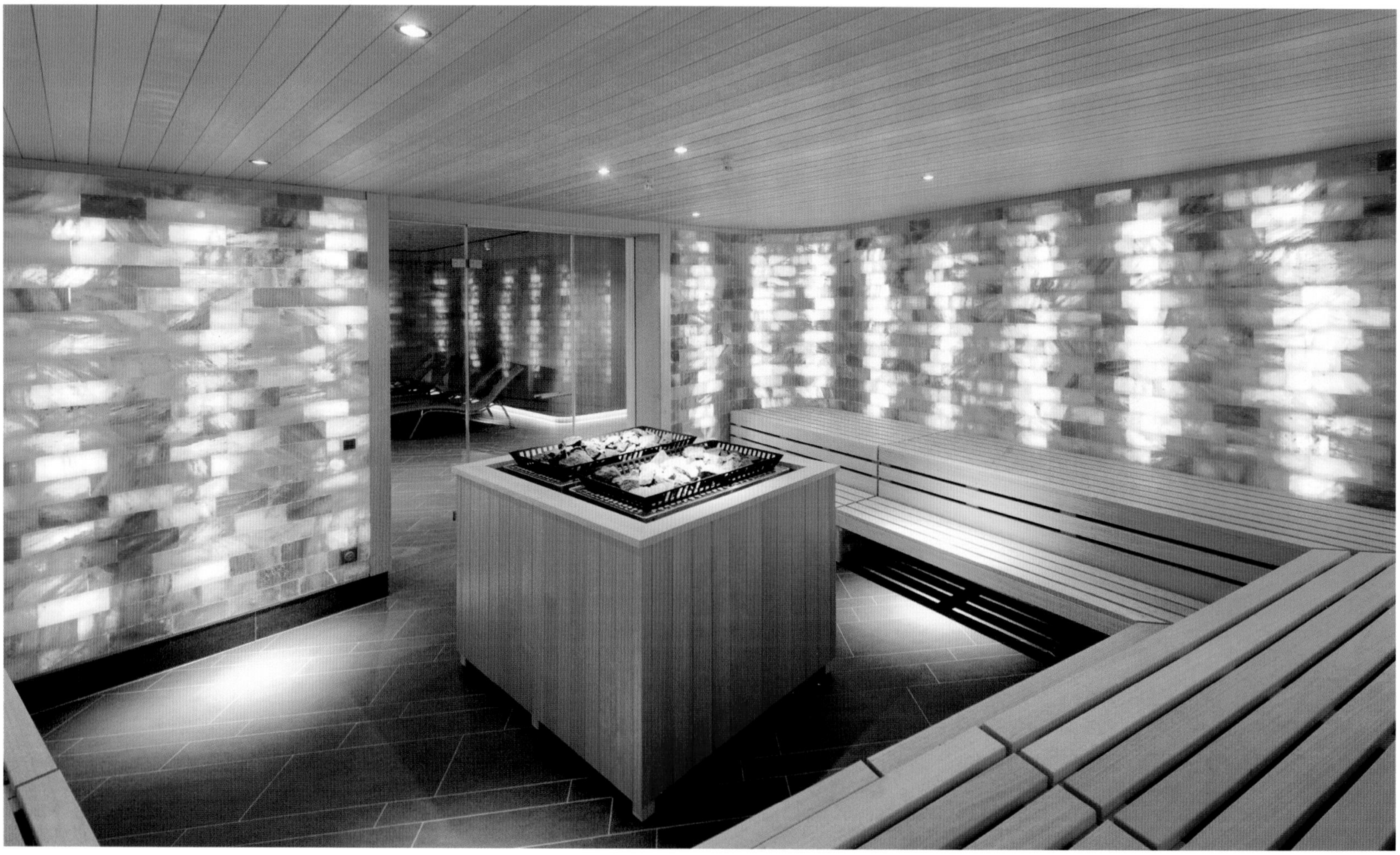

Spa Oryza

Khosla Associates

Design Team: Sandeep Khosla, Amaresh Anand and Lavina Taur
Location: Bangalore
Photography: Pallon Daruwala

The location of the day spa is on one of Bangalore's upmarket yet noisy shopping streets and the designers chose to create an inward looking tropical haven of serenity and tranquility.

Khosla Associates are well established in their style of contemporary tropical residential architecture that blurs the boundaries between inside and outside, and the design at Oryza Spa is an extension of this same sensibility.

The space planning was particularly challenging as the designers had to remodel an existing house structure, breaking walls to free certain zones, adding structural supports and partitions to segregate the public and private spaces and cleverly use all the setbacks as pockets of green visible to the customers from almost every zone.

The spatial planning is linear. On entry one encounters a Balinese water pond replete with lush planting and pebbles that takes you via gentle stepping-stones to the reception. On the left of the reception is an excusive Kerastase Hair Salon, on the right separated by a skin wall are 6 private therapy and treatment rooms each looking via large glass expanses into a private pocket of green planting. To the south of the reception is a polished cement free standing partition that divides the reception from a pedicure and Nail bar and further to the rear of the property are 2 open pavilions for foot reflexology looking inward into another soothing Balinese water feature.

The Designers Sandeep Khosla and Amaresh Anand drew inspiration from the traditional far eastern (Thai, Balinese and Chinese) treatments on offer in the Spa. Natural materials

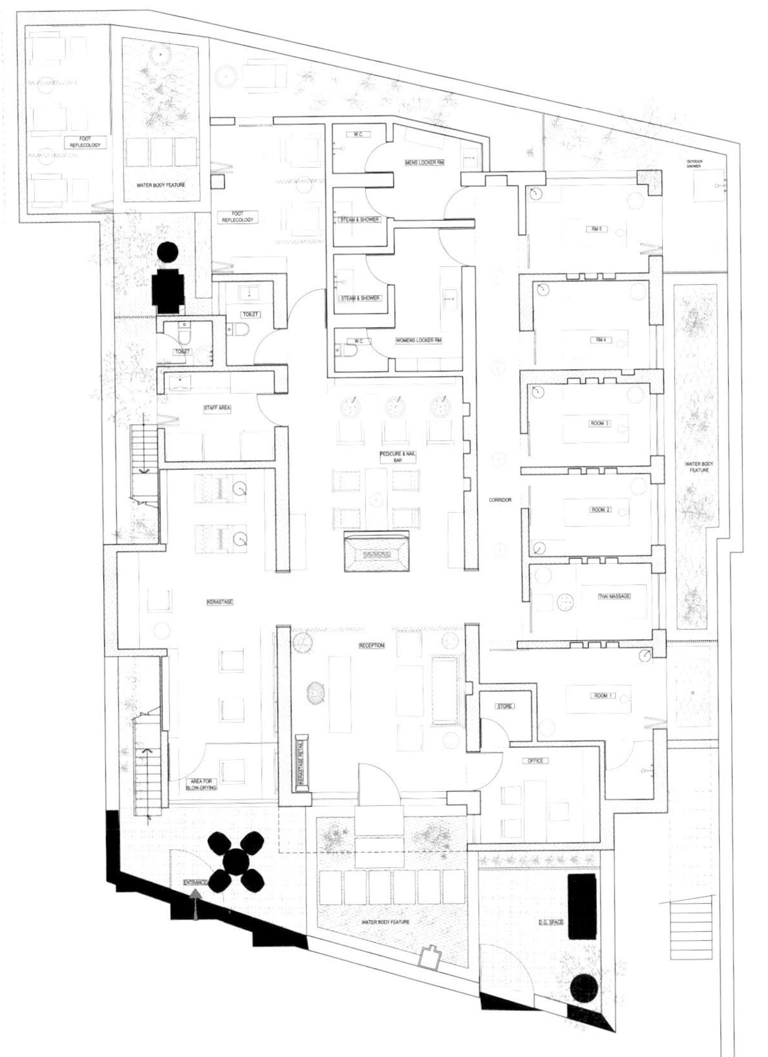
FOOT REFLECOLOGY
WATER BODY FEATURE
W.C.
MENS LOCKER RM
OUTDOOR SHOWER
FOOT REFLECOLOGY
STEAM & SHOWER
RM 5
STEAM & SHOWER
TOILET
RM 4
TOILET
W.C.
WOMENS LOCKER RM
STAFF AREA
ROOM 3
PEDICURE & NAIL BAR
WATER BODY FEATURE
CORRIDOR
ROOM 2
THAI MASSAGE
KERASTASE
RECEPTION
ROOM 1
STORE
OFFICE
KERASTASE RETAIL
AREA FOR BLOW-DRYING
ENTRANCE
WATER BODY FEATURE
D.G. SPACE

oryza

and neutral tones were used to exude a sense of healing and water features were introduced at certain focal points for the same effect. The Architects chose use a back to basics approach with the materials – teak wood floors and polished cement rendered walls offset a bamboo matted ceiling and are further complemented by the stark white upholstery on the seating. The only area that allows colour is the reception, where traditional and contemporary seating is dressed in rich silk upholstery and subtly divided from the rest of the space by sheer curtains.

The treatment rooms lead off from the reception area and privacy is ensured in this zone. A long linear corridor accesses the individual massage rooms and steam/showers and lockers are discreetly tucked in at its end.

Oryza exudes a sense of peace and calm in an otherwise bustling and chaotic city. The tight site conditions prompted efficient space planning. The material usage and rustic textures attempt to connect one closer to nature and with ones senses.

K

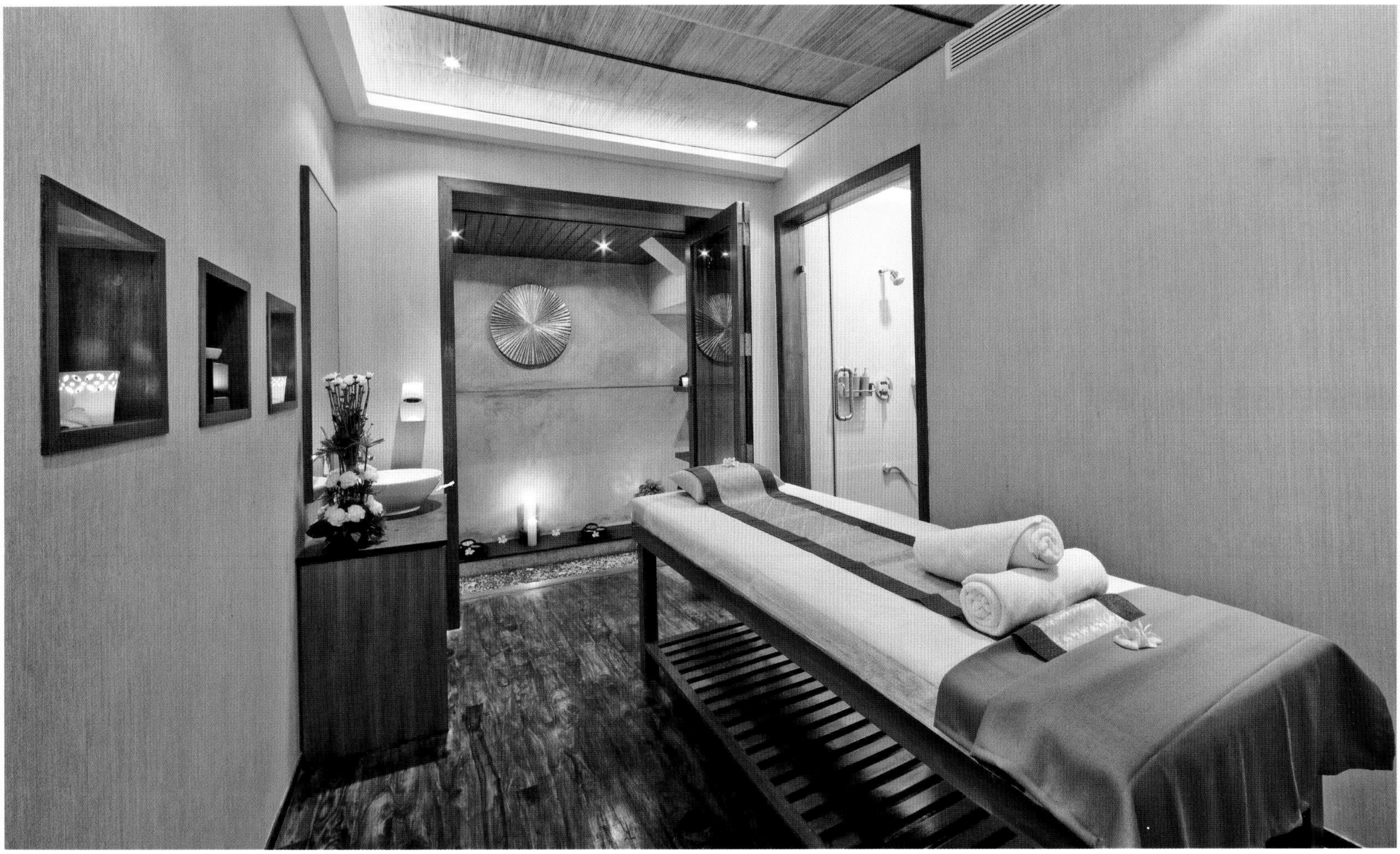

Aura Spa at The Park Hotel, Hyderabad

Khosla Associates

Client: The Park Hotel
Location: Hyderabad
Photography: Bharath Ramamrutham

Khosla Associates were commissioned to design the Park Hotel's Spa "Aura".

A particularly uninspiring space devoid of natural light and ventilation in the basement of the hotel was converted by Khosla Associates into a sparkling environment - inspired by the sheen, transparency, and whiteness of the Golconda Diamond.

The entrance curved corridor walls of the spa were built out of edge polished vertically stacked glass, leading to a circular reception area with a fluid reception counter and brelaxed customer seating sheathed in moulded white resin. A wooden staircase from the pool level also descends into the central womb like reception zone. The stacked glass walls glow from within with LED light giving the surrounding spaces a feeling of lightness.

Surrounding this sparkling central core on the north are the spacious male and female wet areas with locker facilities, change rooms and a large Jacuzzi and Lanconium. On the south is a Gym and a Salon.

Further west from the reception is a spacious transitionary area leading gently to a sensuous curved relaxation area and a series of well appointed therapy rooms and suites. The minimalist transition areas in the spa are peppered with carefully chosen pieces of mirrored organic sculpture by French artist Yahel Chirinian. The reflection of spot lights on these mirrored form deflects onto wall, floor and ceiling surfaces giving an etherial feel to the space.

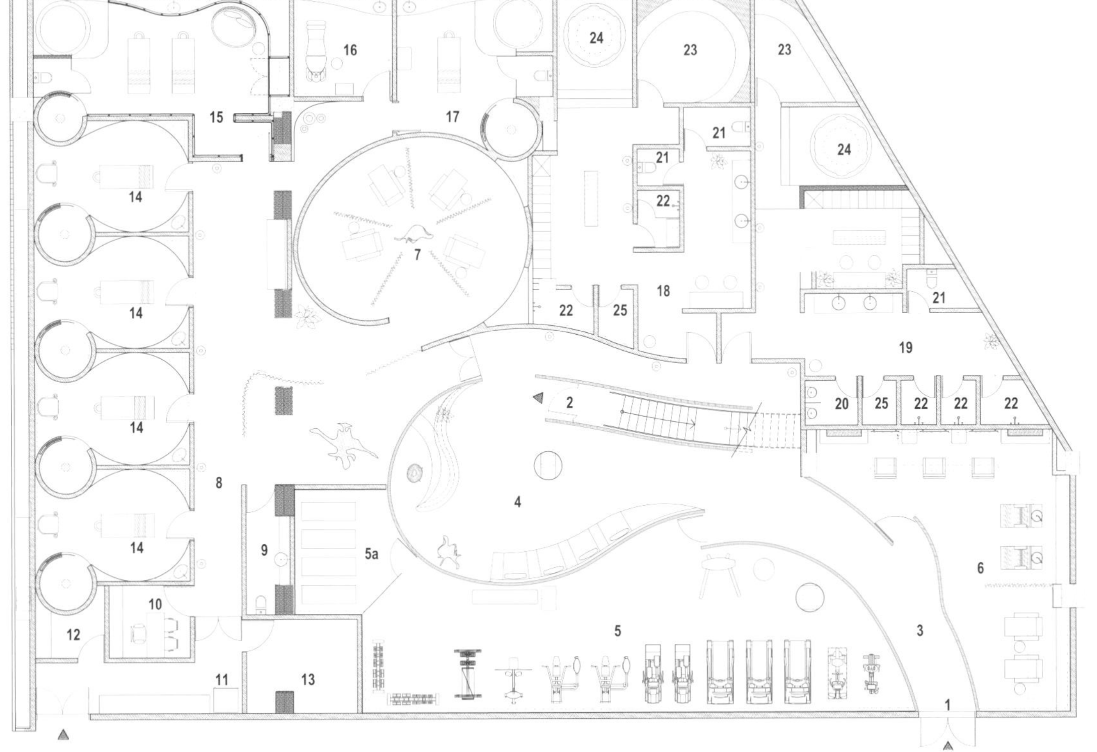

LEGEND

1 MAIN ENTRANCE
2 ENTRANCE FROM POOL
3 CORRIDOR - 1
4 RECEPTION/SEATING
5 GYM
5a YOGA / PILATES
6 SALON
7 RELAXATION/CHROMO THERAPY AREA
8 CORRIDOR - 2
9 WASHROOM
10 MANAGER'S CABIN
11 STAFF PANTRY
12 STORE
13 AHU ROOM
14 THERAPY ROOM
15 COUPLE SUITE-1
16 FACIAL ROOM
17 SUITE-2
18 FEMALE WET AREA
19 MALE WET AREA
20 URINALS
21 W.C
22 SHOWER
23 LACONIUM
24 JACUZZI
25 CHANGE ROOM

The entrance wall and doors of the treatment rooms are clad in an embossed silvern foil, and the curved walls of treatment rooms in a padded diamond shaped pearl white fabric, adding to the feeling of luxury within the space. The futuristic rooms are contrasted with period chairs lending to the space a hint of nostalgia. The circular bathroom capsules are clad with delicate pearl white glass mosaic tiles.

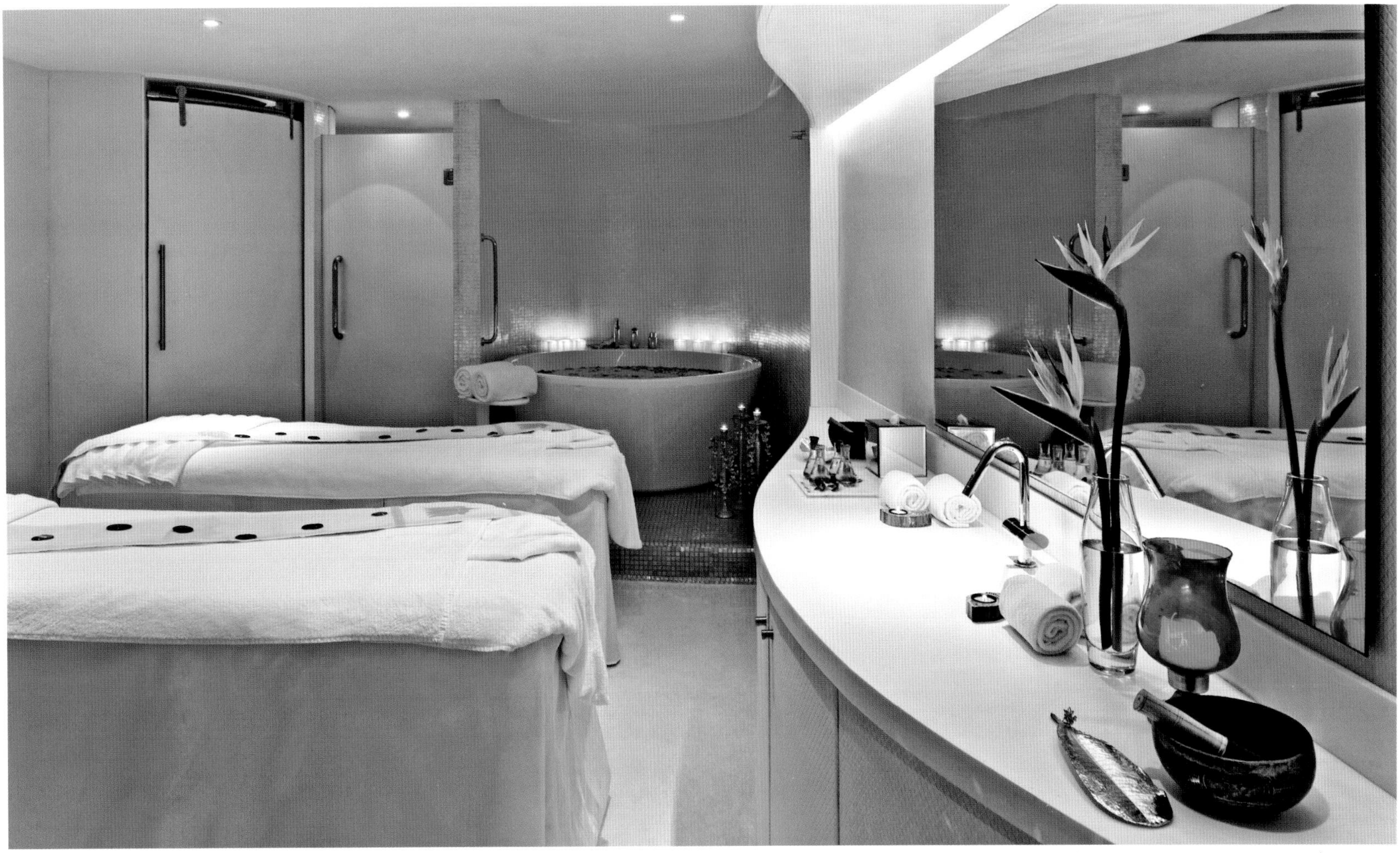

Yi Spa

plajer & franz studio

Client: xix gesellschaft mbh
Location: Berlin
Photography: ken schluchtmann / diephotodesigner.de

Yi Spa is a holistic spirited equilibrated lifestyle-concept: chaste elegance, natural elements like slate stone, mother-of-pearl and dark wood in contrast to coloured glass, exotic plants and delicate fragrances. the idea of Plajer & Franz studio was to make all these elements interplaying distinctively. certain design elements like tone-in-tone gravel between big stoneslabs impose a path through a riverbed in chiang mai and show the correlation between interior design and tradition. Yi offers a piece of imported asian culture integrated into a modern realistic ambiance.

THE SMILE
YOU GIVE
WILL RETURN
TO YOU

A New Roman Spa in Bracciano

PRVS GROUP

Client: private
Location: BRACCIANO, ITALY
Area: 800 m^2

This is a new spa of 800 ms with massage rooms, yoga rooms, and relaxes areas for individuals or free movement. This spa is in a small village, Bracciano, in the center of Italy not too far from Rome (35 km).

The commitment wants to feel this essence and want to transmit to their customers with a new spa that integrates the new modern technologies with the evocation of an ancient spirit!

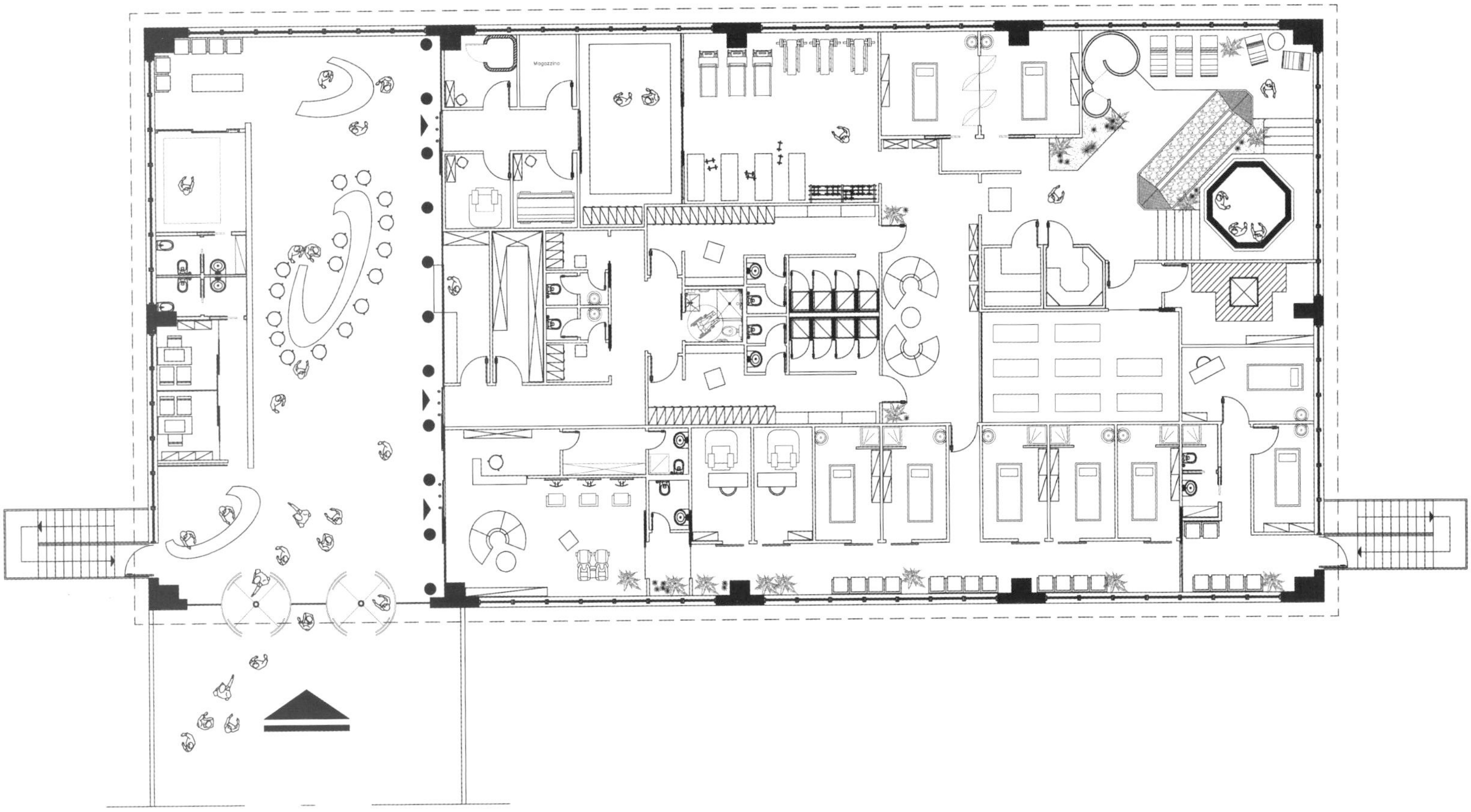

Aveda Lifestyle Salon & Spa – Redchat Kingston

Reis Design

Photography: Tom Lee
Location: Bentalls of Kingston, UK

The Kingston store is the third Lifestyle salon & spa that Reis designed for salon partner Redchat. This site within Bentalls Department store in Surrey marked a radical departure for the brand from the typical high street salon location.

The design incorporates an Aveda retail store, hair salon and beauty spa with 5 treatment rooms.

The design is inspired by Japanese detailing, incorporating a rich palette of natural materials and wooden screening typically associated with Japanese design. The Spa area also incorporates a raised walkway that takes the client on a sensual journey of discovery through the spa and forms a focal point to the relaxation area.

AVEDA
body care
AVEDA
AVEDA
skin care
life style

AVEDA
AVEDA
AVEDA
AVEDA

"Our mission at Aveda is to care for the world we live in, from the products we make to the ways in which we give back to society. At Aveda, we strive to set an example for environmental leadership and responsibility, not just in the world of beauty, but around the world."
–Horst Rechelbacher, founder
AVEDA
AVEDA

AVEDA

Aveda Lifestyle Salon & Spa – Leeds

Reis Design

Photography: Tom Lee
Location: Boar Lane, Leeds, UK
Area: 455 m^2

In partnership with US Hair care brand Aveda, award winning hair stylists, Russell & Robert Eaton have recently opened this flagship Aveda Lifestyle Salon & Spa in Leeds, UK.

Reis Design were briefed to create an urban centre of excellence for hair styling, Ayurvedic beauty therapies and Aveda retail products.

Aveda's commitment to environmental leadership and sustainable development had a strong influence upon the design process. The designers have striven to integrate reclaimed and sustainable materials throughout the project and the scheme takes a low impact strategy in the treatment of this Victorian property in Leeds City centre.

The design makes clever use of specialist lighting to define 'energy' & 'relaxation' areas for the differing salon & spa functions, creating a journey of discovery through the space.

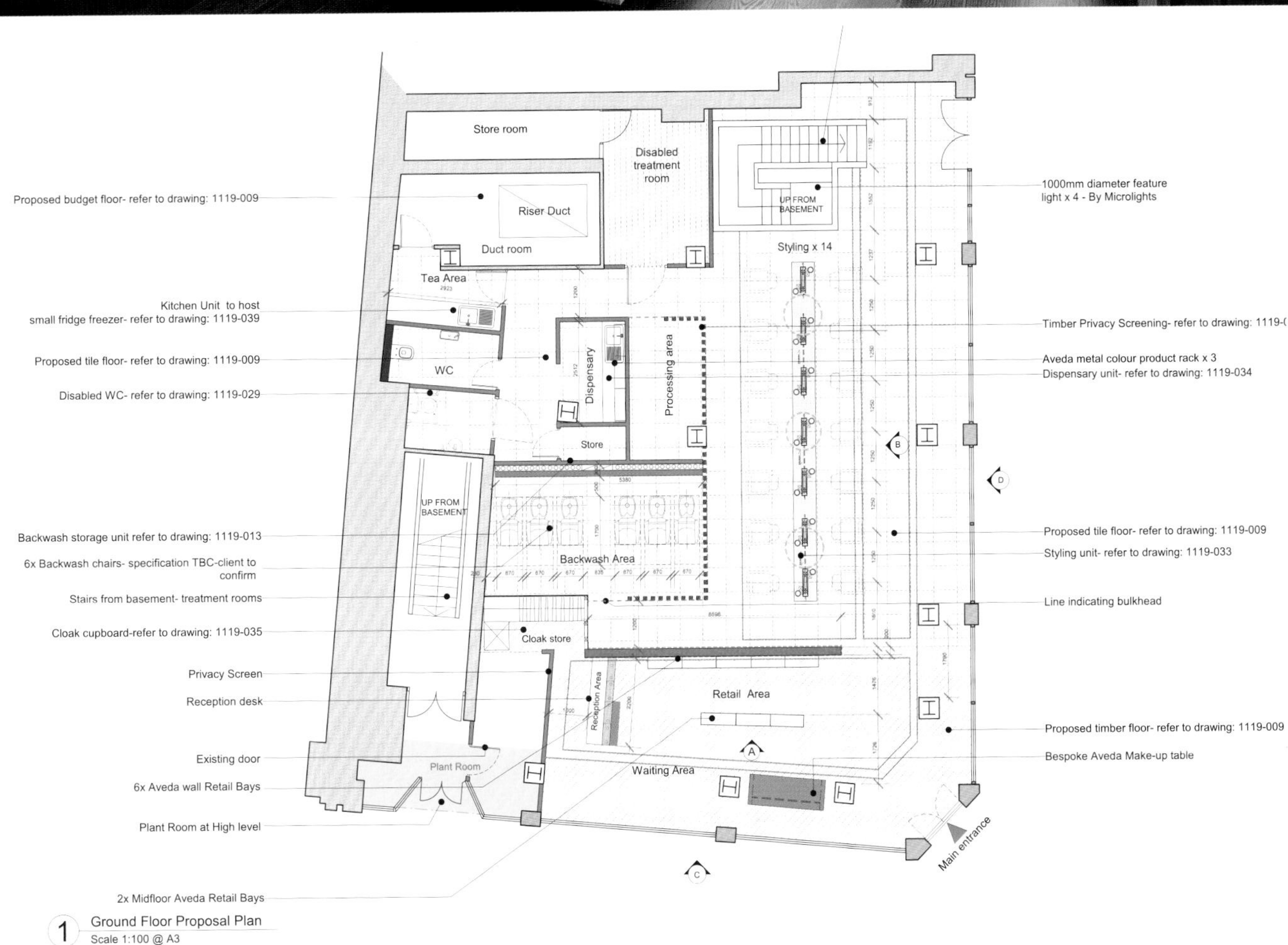

1 Ground Floor Proposal Plan
Scale 1:100 @ A3

our mission at Aveda is to care for the world we live in,
from the products we make to the ways in which we give back to
society. At Aveda, we strive to set an example for environmental
leadership and responsibility, not just in the world of beauty,
but around the world.
— Horst Rechelbacher, founder
life style
fill-ables

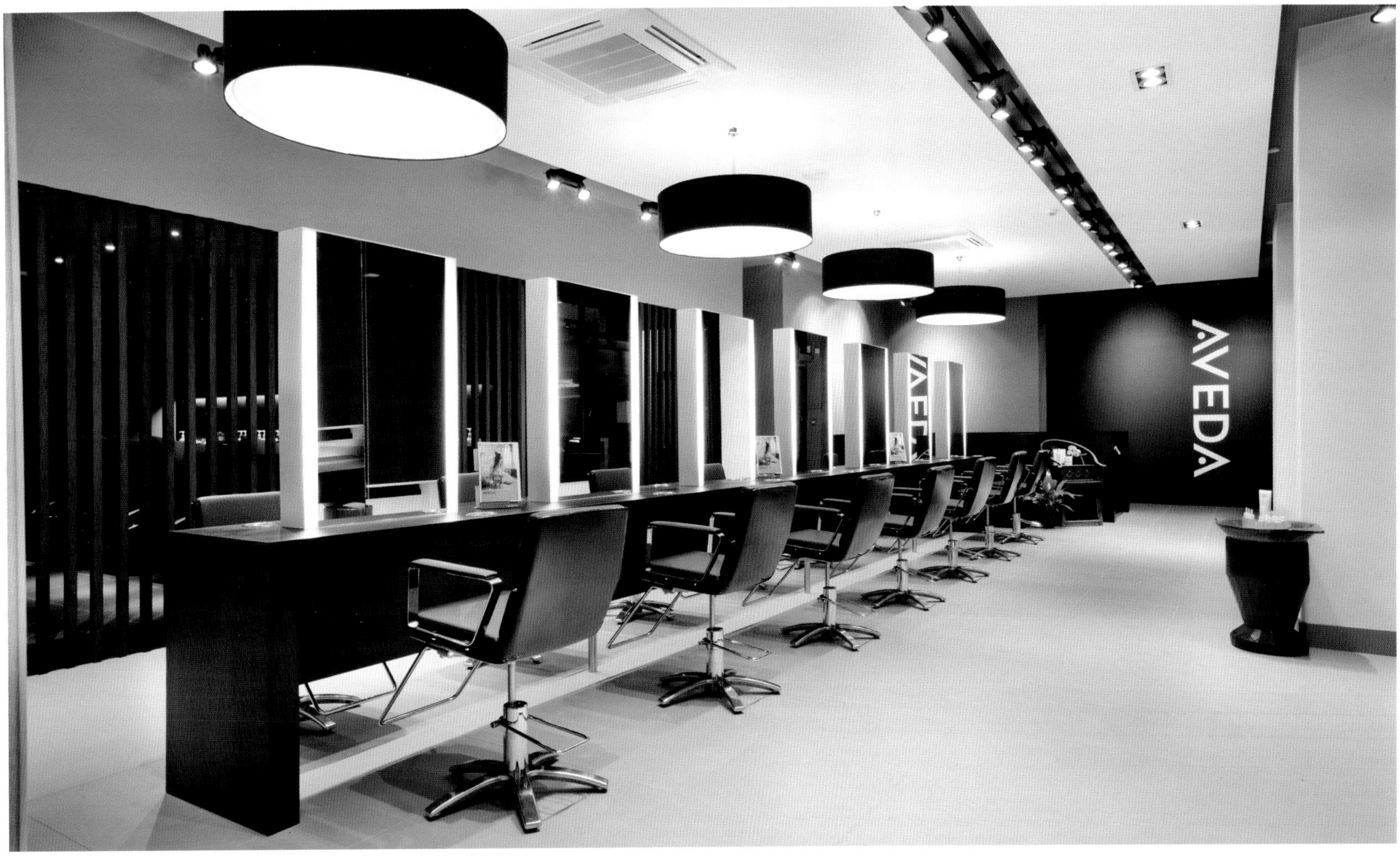
AVEDA

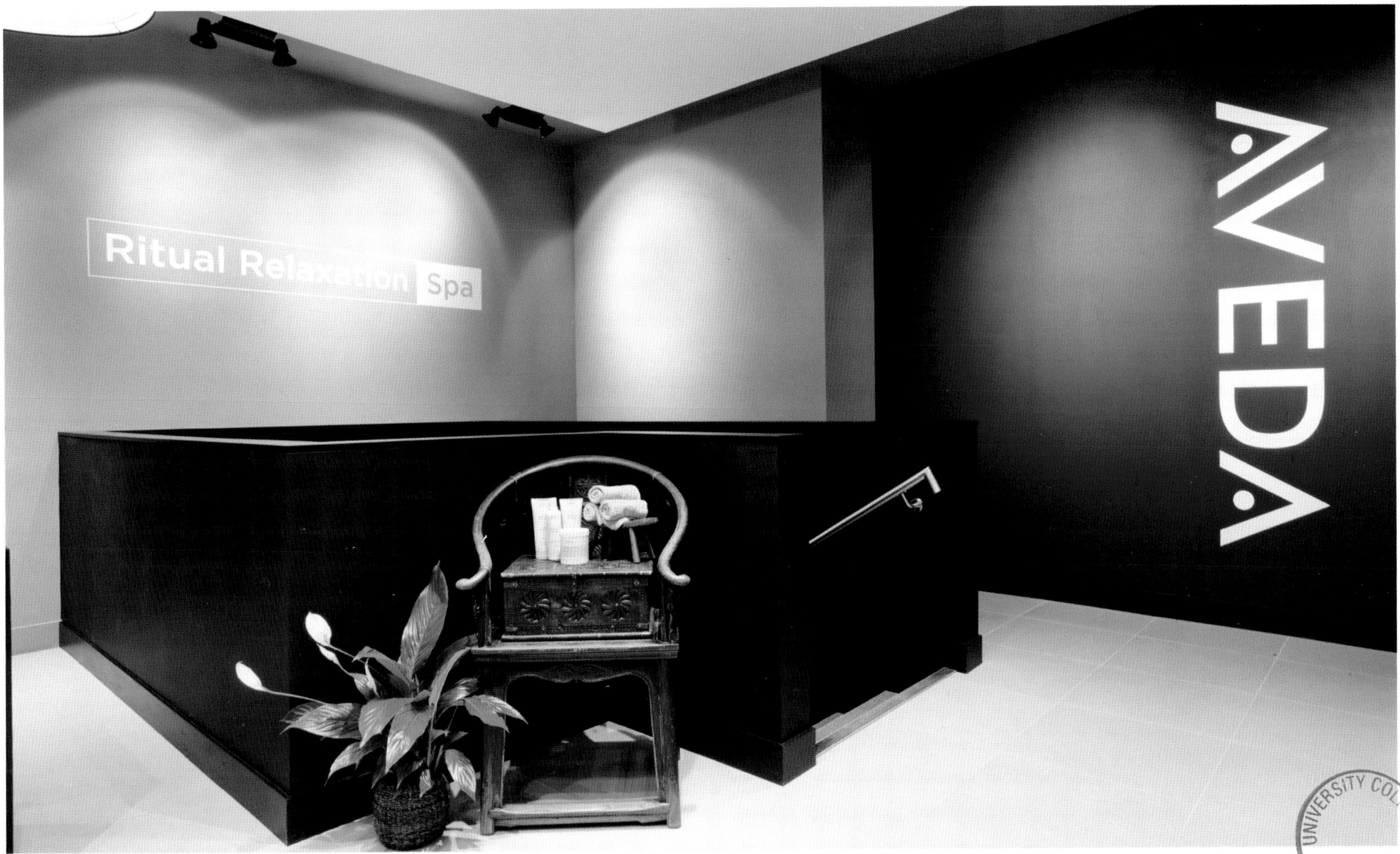
Ritual Relaxation Spa
AVEDA

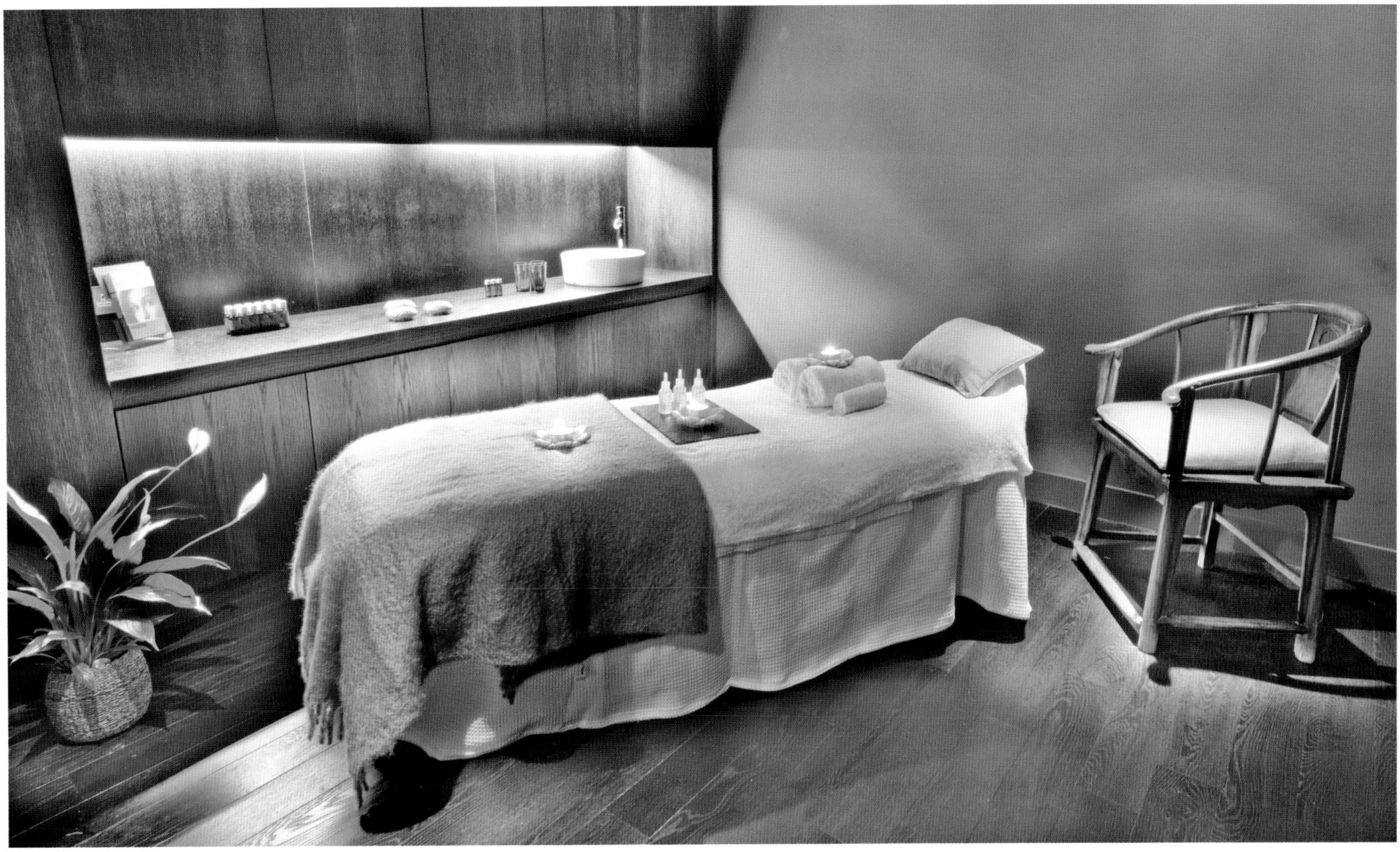

Mahash Natural Day Spa – Moscow

Reis Design

Client: Mahash Salon & Spa
Location: Moscow, Russia
Area: 300 m²

Mahash Natural Day Spa provides a full luxury day spa experience and comprises: Relaxation Cafe & Juice Bar, Retail Store, Hair Salon, Manicure & Pedicure Studio, Yoga Studio, Cosmetology Rooms, Beauty Treatment rooms & Hamam.

Reis Design created the store concept which exists around a central theme of relaxation, utilizing natural materials & burnt color tones combined with an organic graphic motif integrated into store fixtures. A continuous 'Ribbon' ceiling feature defines the customer journey of exploration through 'energy' and 'relaxation' zones defined within the store.

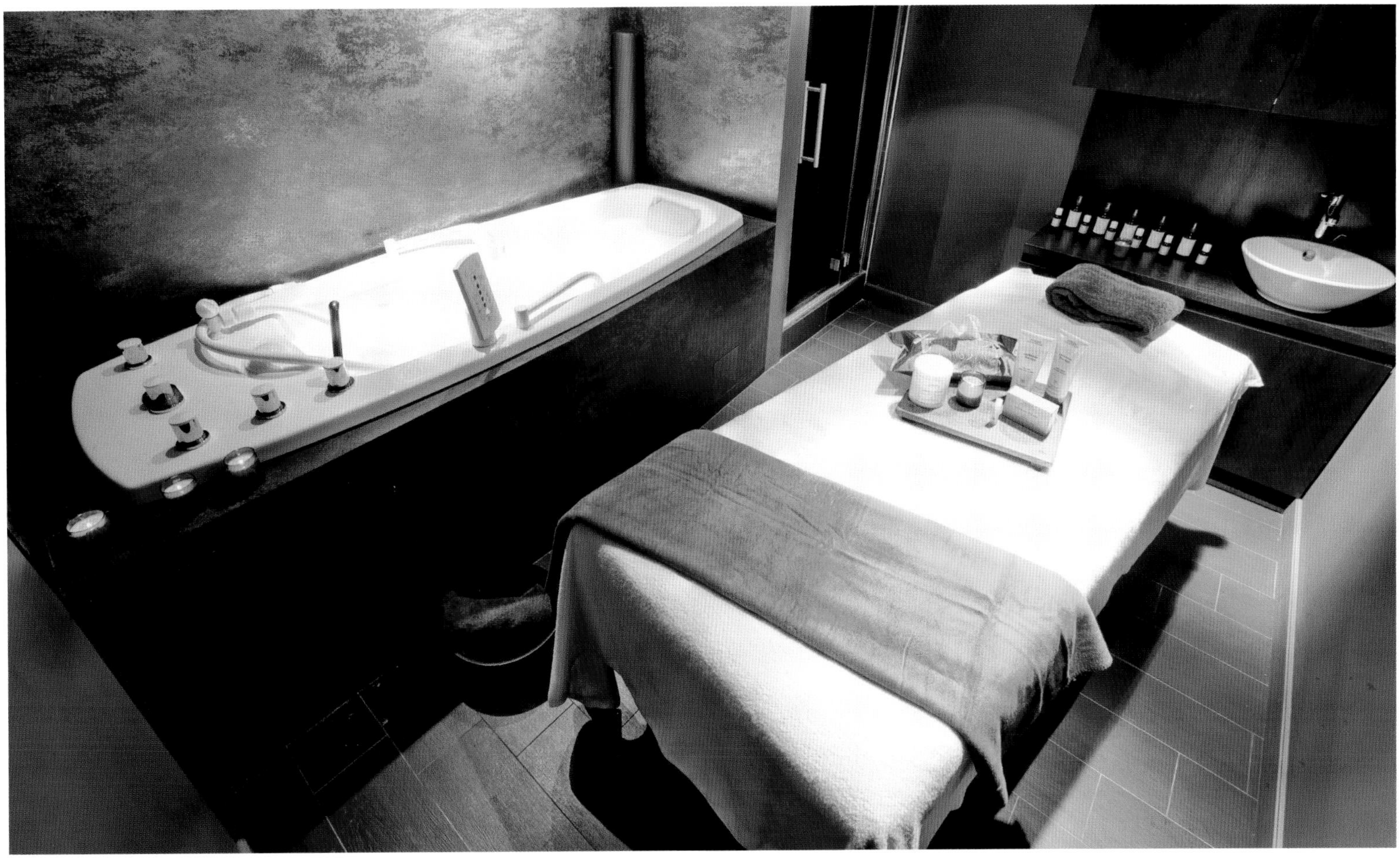

AVEDA
caribbean therapy
BODY CREME
CRÈME POUR LE CORPS
AVEDA
caribbean therapy
BODY CLEANSER
AVEDA
caribbean therapy
BATH BAR
AVEDA
caribbean therapy
BODY SCRUB
15.8 oz/450 g

The Chuan Spa, The Langham Hotel, London

Richmond International

Client: The Langham Hotel
Location: London, UK

The Chuan Spa concept balances the five elements of wood, fire, earth, metal and water to enhance physical and mental wellbeing.

The challenge was to incorporate the oriental values of the Chuan into a Grade Two listed Banking Hall. The main hall features the Reception area and "Contemplation" zone, which was created as a freestanding element within the space so as not to impact on the existing structure. Padded panels and bespoke relaxation beds offer an aura of calm, while a fire sculpture, custom-designed in black granite and black iron, provides a contemplative focal point.

On the way to the treatment rooms, guests pass through a "Moongate", a signature element of the Chuan Spa, designed as a broken portal in textured metals to give a more contemporary feel.

The six treatment rooms reflect the Oriental elements of the Chuan brand, with a dark seductive palette of bronze, crimson, black and copper, while the natural finishes to the floors and walls are restricted to dark timber, slate and specialist shell wall coverings. These finishes continue into the exclusive Couple's Spa Suite which features a solid timber soaking tub.

The Jacuzzi, Salt Room and heated relaxation benches are located on the lower ground floor and the finishes were upgraded with a palette of black stone and marble mosaics, creating a sophisticated and relaxing ambiance. In the pool, a design highlight of the Spa, dark textural stone walls are dramatically lit and a bespoke decorative tree motif panel provides a focal interest.

Bota Bota, Spa-sur-l'eau

Sid Lee Architecture

Client: Bota Bota, Spa-sur-l'eau
Location: Montreal

In addition to the wide range of treatments offered, the Bota Bota experience immerses visitors in an environment that plays host to both light and dark. The Sid Lee Architecture team set out to create an indoor space conducive to introspection and an outdoor space affording spectacular views of the city, from the upper decks. Visitors forget they're on a boat as they transition through the five different levels, discovering the city from each one.

The closer the spaces are to the water, the darker and more intimate they are; the closer they are to nature, the more impressive the views of the horizon. The relation between these two extremes comes thanks to the 678 portholes that dot the boat, allowing daylight to penetrate the treatment rooms. As such, the transition from water to sky, and dark to light, is made possible.

Bota Bota's identity: marine markers

This concept is veritably unique and its brand image unlike any other. Using a visual language characterized by pure, simple lines, the spa brings markers of the marine world to its logo, signage and stationery.

Technical challenges

The uniqueness of the Bota Bota, spa-sur-l'eau project is due to the fact that many fields of expertise were brought together. The project represents a fusion of disciplines: building architecture, naval architecture, interior design, industrial design, as well as building and naval engineering.

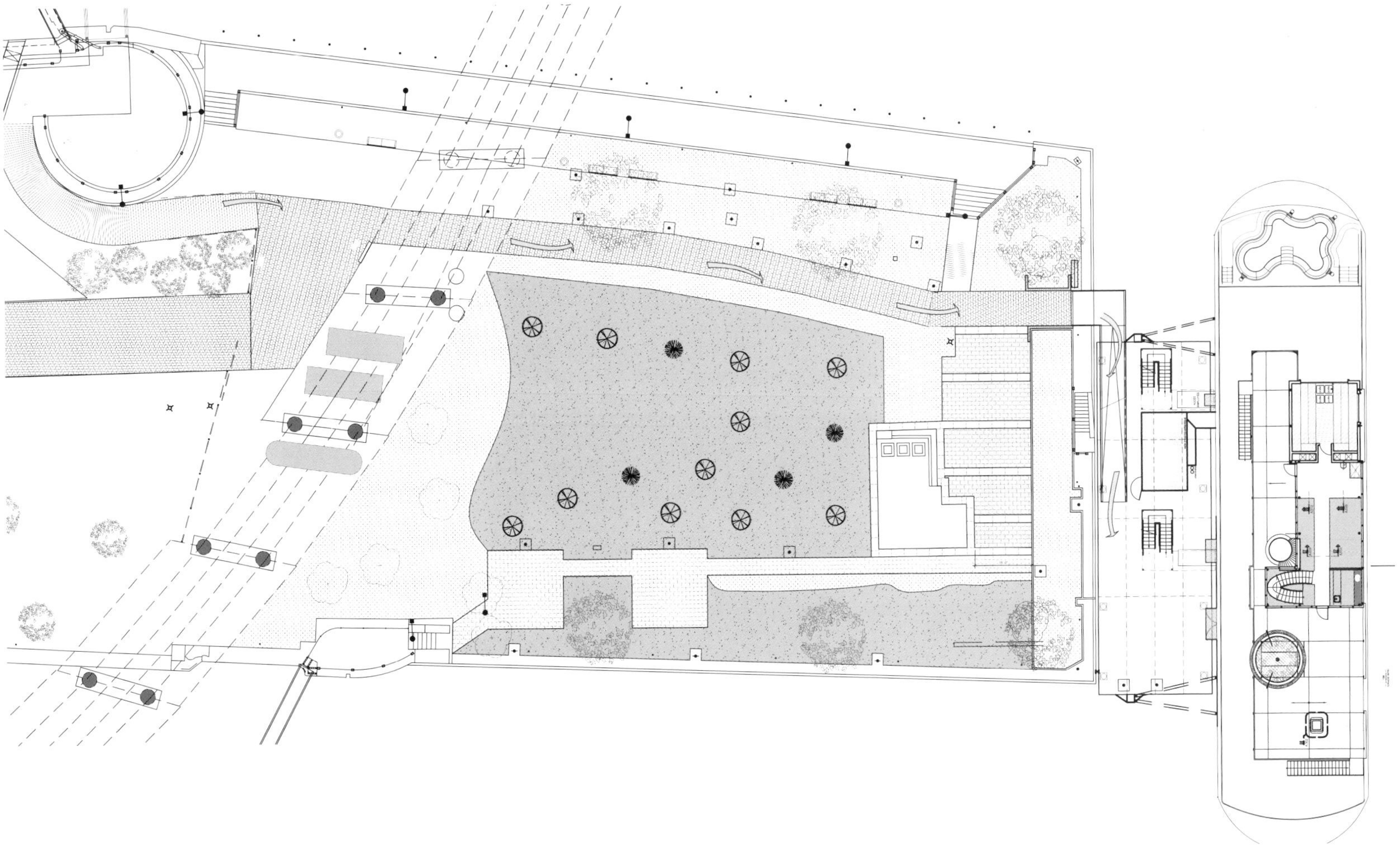

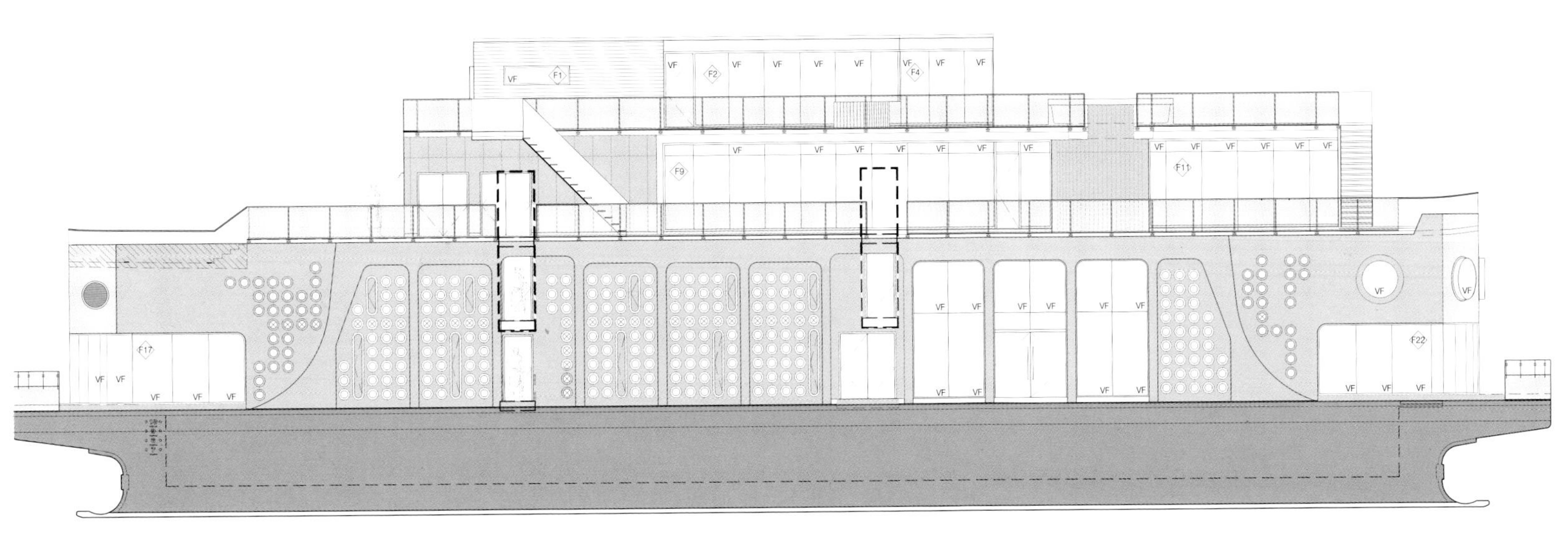
F1
F2
F4
F9
F11
F17
F22
VF

3
PONT
PROMENADE
SAUNA FLEUVE
BAIN VAPEUR
BAIN FROID
TERRASSES
DOUCHES
TOILETTES

2
PONT
4
3
2
1
0

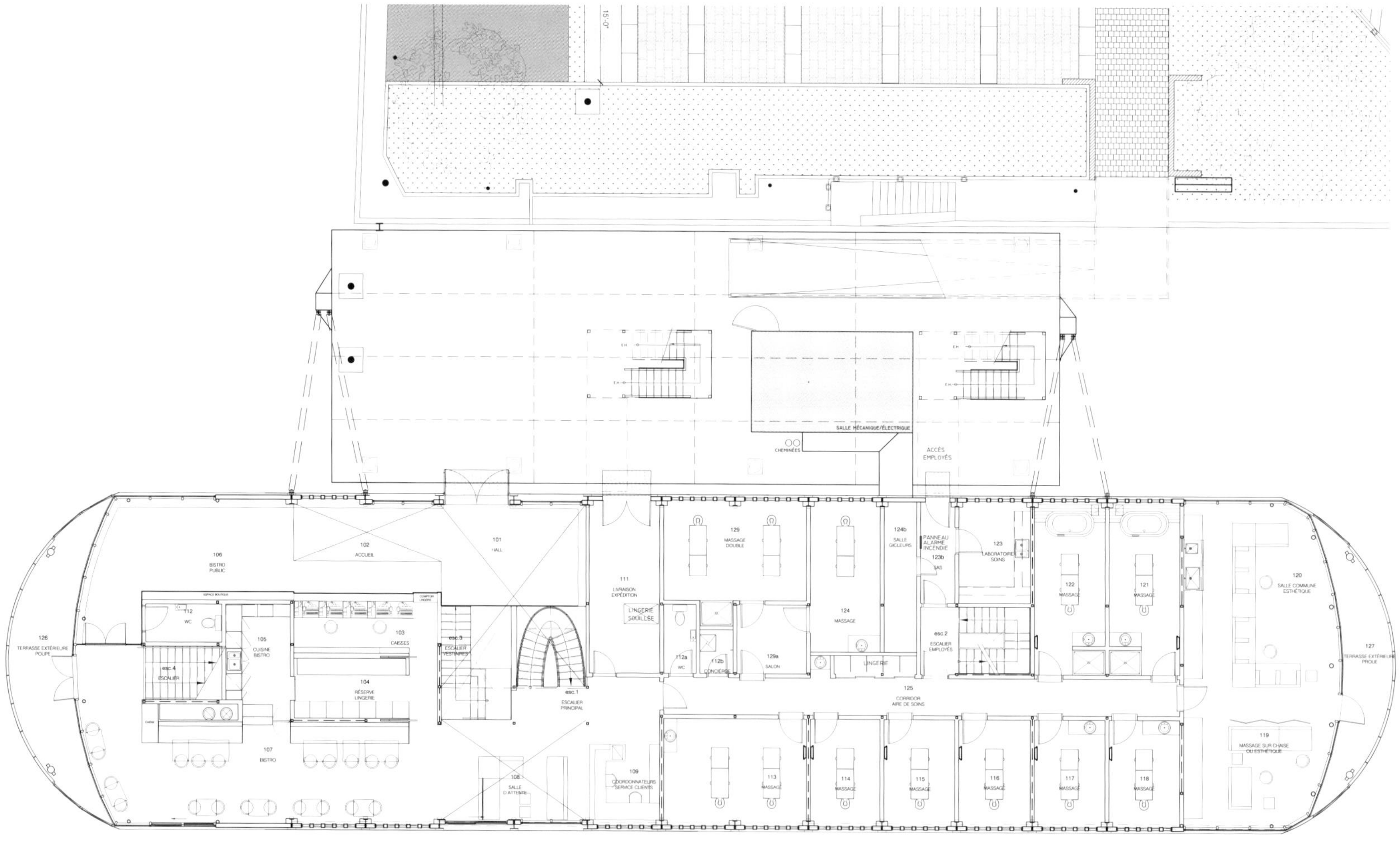

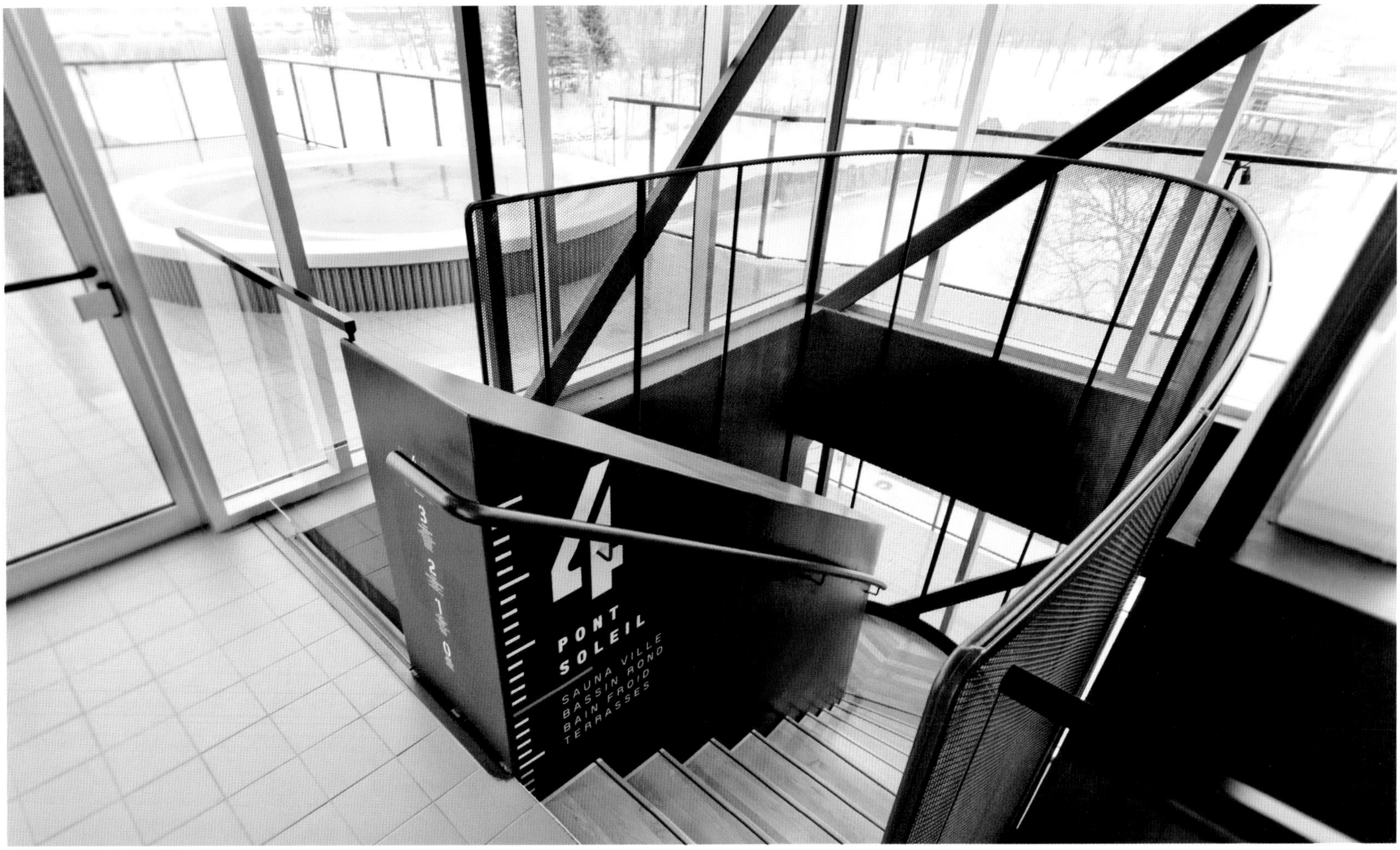
4
PONT
SOLEIL
SAUNA VILLE
BASSIN ROND
BAIN FROID
TERRASSES

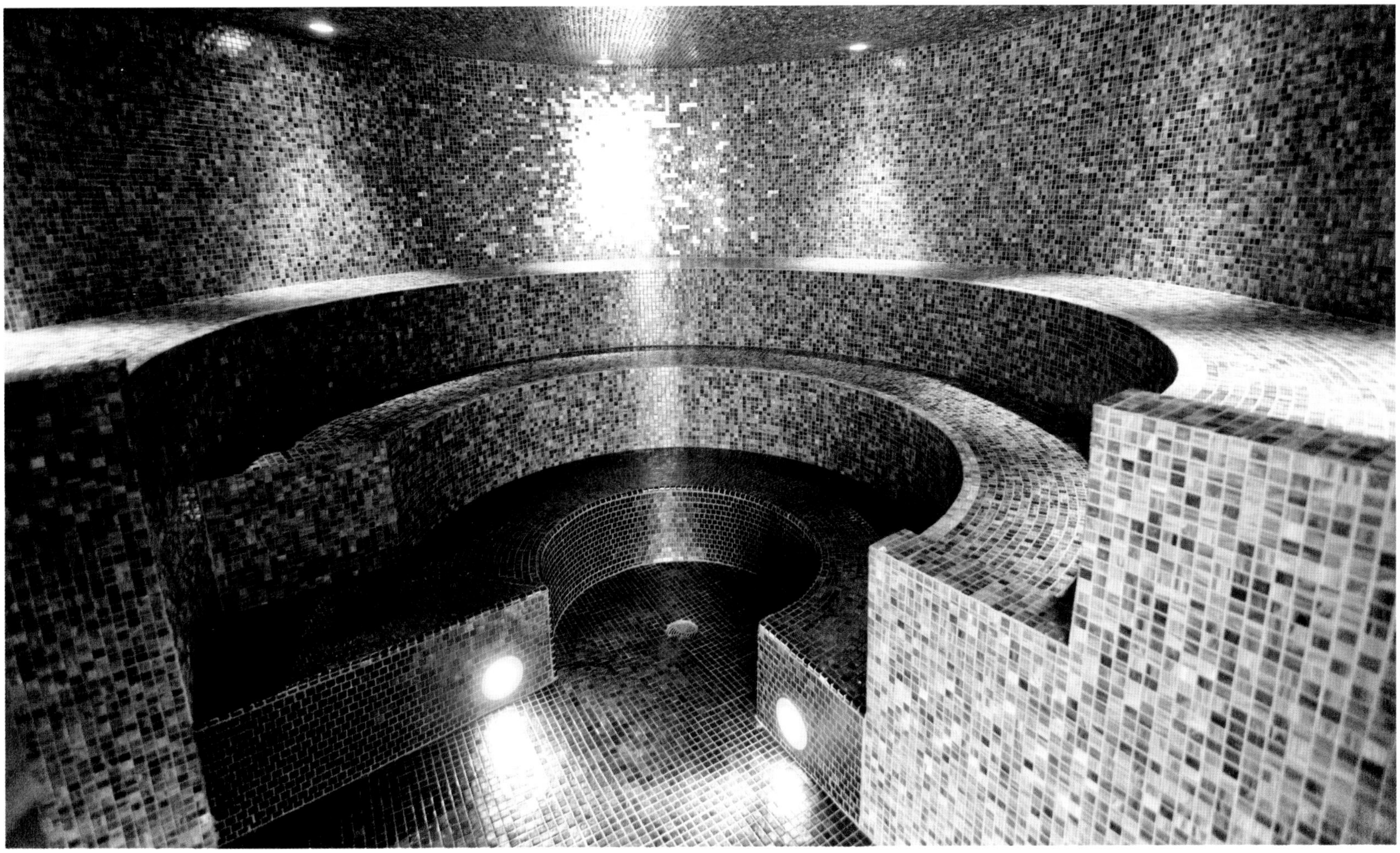

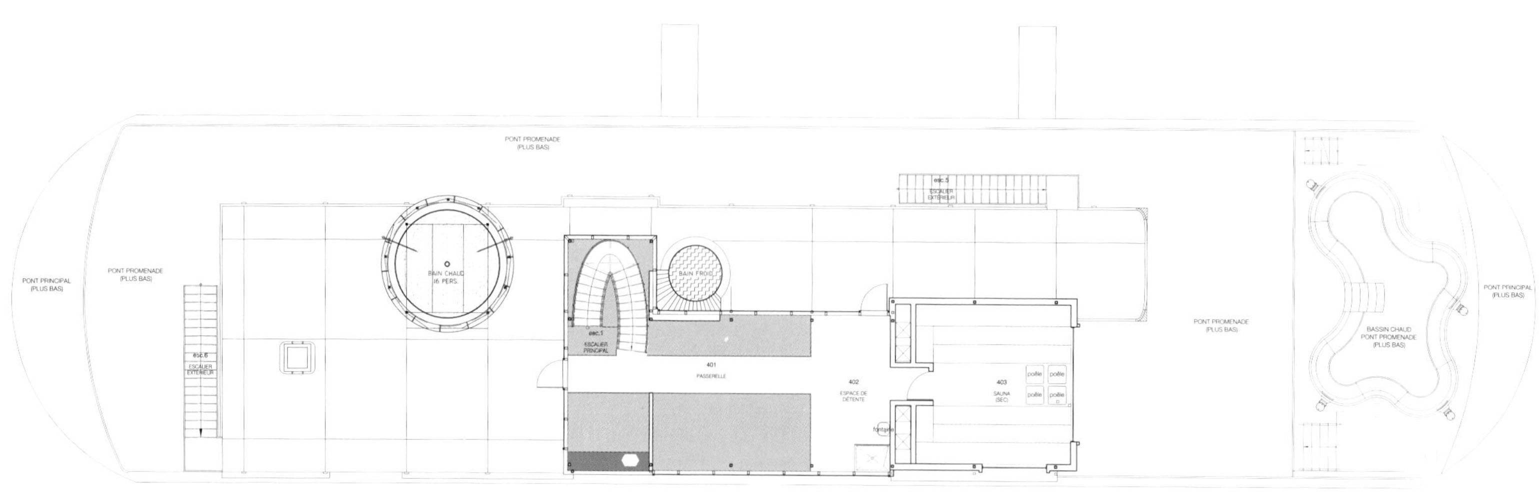
PONT PROMENADE
(PLUS BAS)
PONT PRINCIPAL
(PLUS BAS)
PONT PROMENADE
(PLUS BAS)
esc.6
ESCALIER
EXTÉRIEUR
BAIN CHAUD
16 PERS.
esc.1
ESCALIER
PRINCIPAL
BAIN FROID
401
PASSERELLE
esc.5
ESCALIER
EXTÉRIEUR
402
ESPACE DE
DÉTENTE
fontaine
403
SAUNA
(SEC)
poêle
poêle
poêle
poêle
PONT PROMENADE
(PLUS BAS)
BASSIN CHAUD
PONT PROMENADE
(PLUS BAS)
PONT PRINCIPAL
(PLUS BAS)

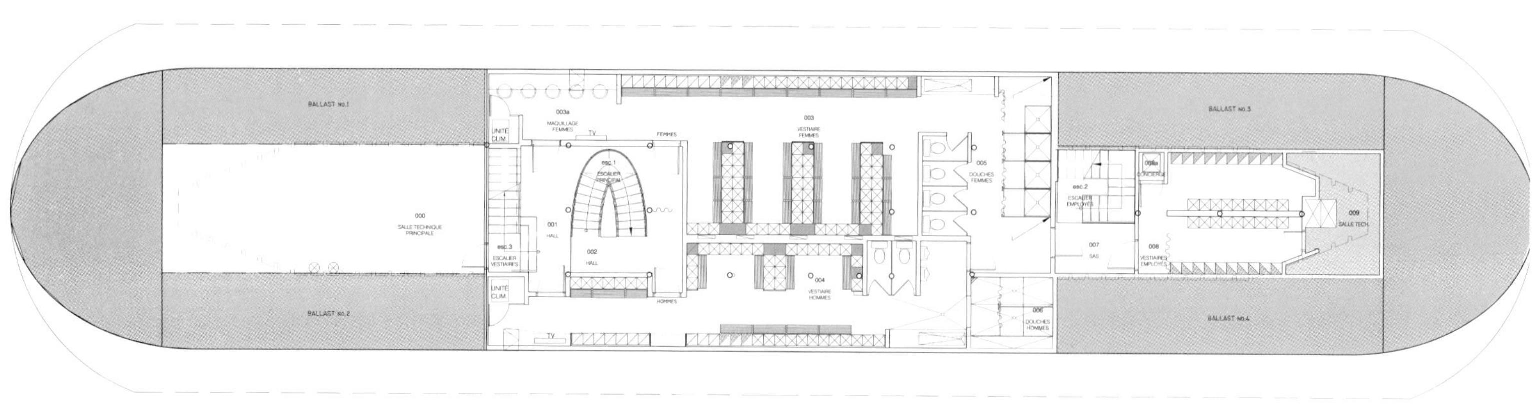
BALLAST NO.1
000
SALLE TECHNIQUE
PRINCIPALE
BALLAST NO.2
UNITÉ
CLIM
esc.3
ESCALIER
VESTIAIRES
UNITÉ
CLIM
003a
MAQUILLAGE
FEMMES
TV
FEMMES
esc.1
ESCALIER
PRINCIPAL
001
HALL
002
HALL
HOMMES
TV
003
VESTIAIRE
FEMMES
004
VESTIAIRE
HOMMES
005
DOUCHES
FEMMES
006
DOUCHES
HOMMES
esc.2
ESCALIER
EMPLOYÉS
007
SAS
CONCIERGE
008
VESTIAIRES
EMPLOYÉS
009
SALLE TECH.
BALLAST NO.3
BALLAST NO.4

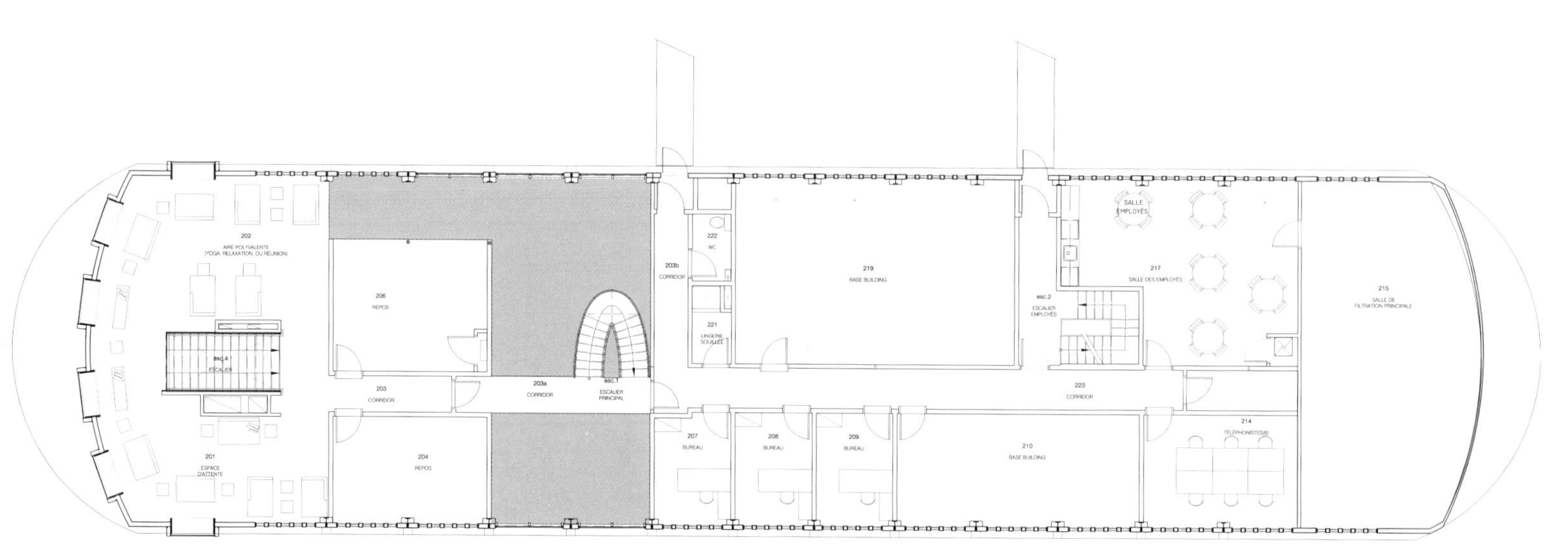
202
AIRE POLYVALENTE
(YOGA, RELAXATION, OU RÉUNION)
esc.4
ESCALIER
201
ESPACE
D'ATTENTE
206
REPOS
203
CORRIDOR
204
REPOS
203a
CORRIDOR
esc.1
ESCALIER
PRINCIPAL
222
WC
203b
CORRIDOR
221
LINGERIE
SOUILLÉE
207
BUREAU
208
BUREAU
209
BUREAU
219
BASE BUILDING
esc.2
ESCALIER
EMPLOYÉS
223
CORRIDOR
210
BASE BUILDING
SALLE
EMPLOYÉS
217
SALLE DES EMPLOYÉS
214
TÉLÉPHONISTES(6)
215
SALLE DE
FILTRATION PRINCIPALE

Wellness Lone

Studio 92

Designer: Robert Dragogna, Ester Miletic
Location: Rovinj, Croatia
Client: Abilia d.d.
Floor Area: 1,700 m^2
Built Area: 1,300 m^2
Photography: Rajan Milosevic

Located in Rovinj (Croatia), the Wellness and Spa Lone project is part of Hotel Lone, which is the first Design Hotel in Croatia. The development of spa businesses has been booming all over Croatia over the last few years giving us a possibility, as a mayor Spa design company in the county, to experiment with different design processes. The principal of minimalistic aesthetic present in the hotel inspired a contemporary, natural approach towards the Spa Lone, where the space design emphasizes extreme leisure and comfort with an artistic note.

The entire Spa is conceived as a spatial continuum connecting various functions, such as indoor pool, gym, sauna centre, hydro-massage pool and treatment rooms, creating a link – a corridor where you can relax, experience cromotherapy on a long colored wall or just pass through enjoying the outdoor view.

Throughout the interior, basic white and black tones are applied, emphasizing the material and its texture. Black glass panels contrast with dark granulated ceramic on the floor, while white, shiny Barisol membrane illuminated with RGB light reflects scratched Italian marble. These basic colors match perfectly with wide Barisol wall and ceiling, which give the interior almost a surreal atmosphere with its multicolored surface. Wooden panels in treatment rooms give a soft and natural touch to the interior, almost anticipating the touch of a therapist on a client's body.

Each part of the interior was designed and made in situ and each material carefully chosen. The entire design was completed with Italian Moroso brand furniture, designed by Patricia Urquiola. Sculptured vases are designed by the British designer, Ron Arad. Each detail is intended to create a sense of chic comfort and silence, giving clients a unique experience and a meticulous spa touch.

Aqua

Hotel Belvedere and Spa

Studio Bizzarro & Partners

Client: Hotel Belvedere
Location: Riccione, Italy
Photography: Alberto Bravini

The studio has made every room a unique location because of colors, disposition and decoration, but keeping a stylistic coherence to give a unitary image to the hotel and give it a univocal connotation. The style is researched, cozy but contemporary.

The use of natural and easy-maintenance materials has been decided to ensure a very low wear level in time.

As a background to the wadded bed-heads of king size beds, soft curtains and wallpaper appear and play on the lowest tone variations of white: everything is lighted by the use of colored accessories – from violet to sky-blue, from brown to silver.

Rooms and suites have been thought to answer the different needs of the users that attend the hotel during different periods of the year: from a couple that stops in winter for a wellness week end, to a group of bikers who ventures in Rimini's hills in spring and autumn, to the family who stays for a week or two in the summer. In this sense, then, the spaces' organization and the permeation among the rooms, together with the project of every single furnishing element – from beds, to sofas, from closets to besides tables – correspond to the versatility criteria that Hotel Belvedere wants to pursue offering that completeness and complexity of solutions suitable and adaptable to every season and customer.

Olywell

Studio Bizzarro & Partners

Location: Naple, Italy

Oliwell is a Wellness Club realized inside Vulcano Buono, a building planned by Renzo Piano. It is organized in a series of wellness areas that are innovative and evocative, devoted to fitness and beauty and planned following cutting-edge criteria, based on qualitative standards that are unique for Central-Southern Italy.

Oliwell overlooks one of the squares of the internal pathway, directly receiving light from the wide central surface which represents the crater of Vesuvius. When strolling in the square you can immediately feel its presence, thanks to its long screens that unveil the full equipment of the weight room and the powerful graphic messages that suggest a philosophy aiming to regain the psychological and physical daily balance. The entrance is cosy but its message is powerful: thanks to the brand it becomes a philosophy of one's own behaviour, almost like a mission's flag. The entrance is large, with a clear organizational logic which finds its distributive fulcrum in the reception, realized in dark wood. The spacious hall merges with the lounge and restaurant area, dominated by the multi-coloured cloud of lights.

Red, beige and brown are the dominant colours that perfectly melt in the clear stone of the floors. This is a recurring colour theme in the whole Club, almost dramatic in the relation with floor, walls and furnishing, which are pleasantly reflected by a graphic which, thanks to its out-of-scale dimension panels, sends involving multi-coloured messages on neutral backgrounds of matter. A wide and complex distribution axis easily guides the flow of users towards the locker rooms and, from here, to the several activity rooms, the pools and the Thermarium. The lighting emphasizes and drives the attention to pathways and places, caressing the surfaces and giving the users involving emotional clues.

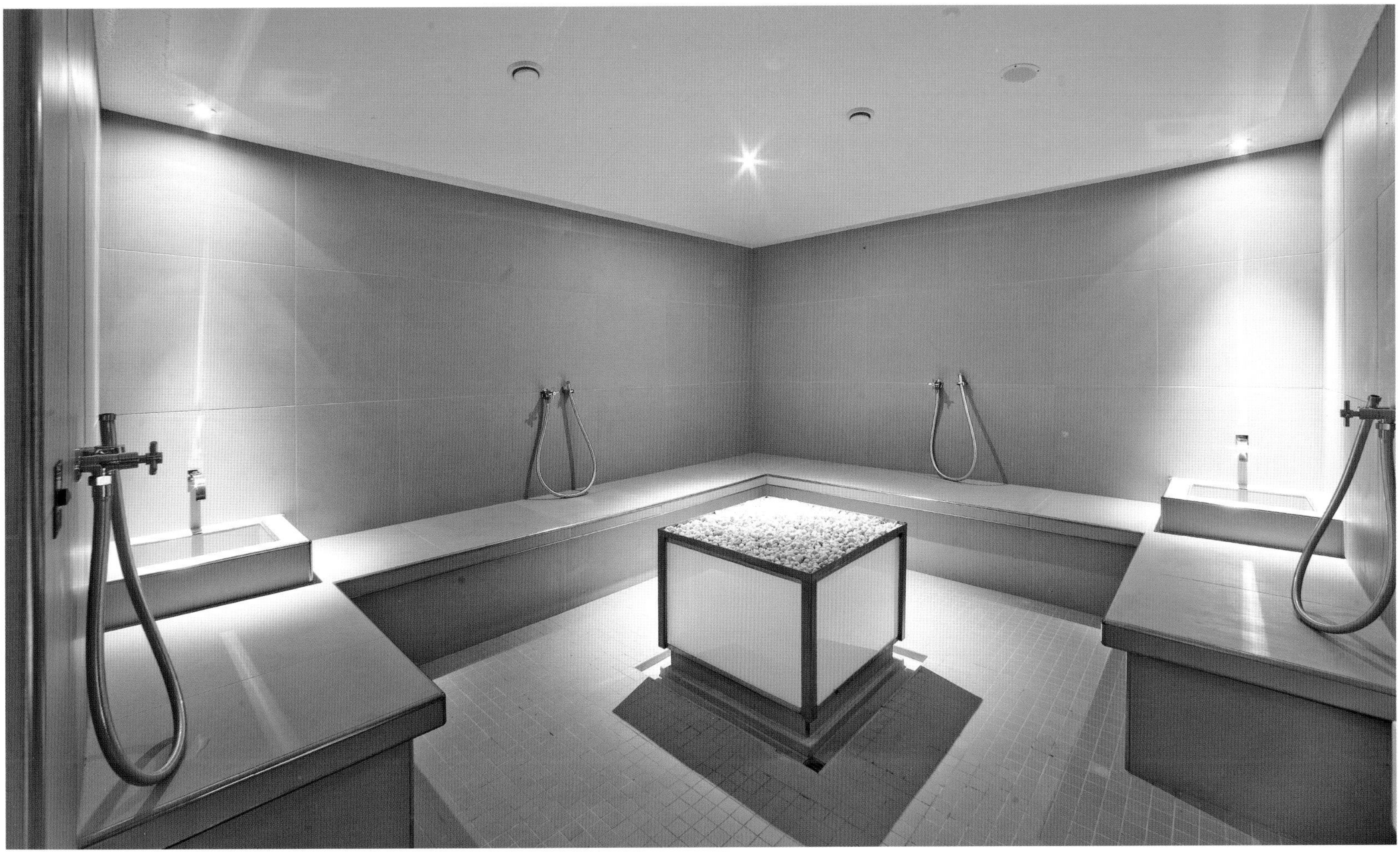

Get Fit City Club

Studio Matteo Nunziati

Location: Milan, Italy

The Studio Matteo Nunziati realized and coordinated, in all its phases, the project Get Fit City Club. The main inspiration comes from the asymmetric, monumental simplicity of the roman Lombard, besides the artificial channels, the navigli.

The space was conceptualized as an internal courtyard of an abbey, where one could take rest and recover, finding comfort and protection from the whirling rhythms of the contemporary metropolis. For this reason, natural materials like stone, ceramics, wood and leather were used, composed with paths of water and light which has been studied particularly.

At the lower floor you find the spa. The spa has been divided in small spaces, each of them analyzed and planned to the smallest detail. The Sauna is characterized by ceiling illuminated by Swarovski crystals and by red-hot lava stone niche, where water falls to generate the vapour. The Thalasso therapy has comfortable backlit mosaic benches. In the Turkish bath created in stone has a small reaction bath, also completely covered in lava stone. The Whirlpool is entirely in stone and has comfortable reserved places where one can relax.

The Massage rooms are also covered in stone, marked by a band in teak wood that follows continuously from floor to ceiling. There is the possibility to create different scenarios of light, to modify the perception of the space in relation to the treatments carried out.

Victoria Gardens

Studio Matteo Nunziati

Location: Beijing, China

Every person has available to their use a private suite, a completely younique place with all the benefits of a spa (sauna, steam, whirlpool bath, massage, etc.).

The main inspiration for this project was Chinese art tradition. The chosen decors and materials suggest a dialog between the place and the local culture while keeping a distinctive contemporary mark.

Life Spa, the Empire Hotels & Resorts, Hong Kong

Tom Hisano

Location: Causeway Bay, Hong Kong
Photography: Victor Lam Studio
Area: 2,200 m^2

Life SPA is located on 5/F in newly converted high-rise hotel near Victoria Park, Hong Kong, specially catering for Life Style floor guest of 56 rooms. Normally, lowest floors of hotel are sold at the cheapest rate, especially building is surrounded by local old buildings, but Life Style floors are sold at more than double rate, thanks to Life SPA package to business travelers.

The SPA adapts concept design, applying 5 elements of Chinese traditional brief, elements on globe – Metal, Wood, Water, Fire & Earth, which are used as healing, and materialized by most advanced technology SPA machines from Europe and Japan, such as Oxygen Capsule, Dr. Sauna, Bedrock Capsule, from Japan, Water bed Massager from Germany, Steam & Light healing Capsule from Italy. All shower rooms are using Rain Forest Shower with massage function and color therapy.

Space is divided into 6 healing rooms and main reception with relaxation space, where guest can view green podium garden and the garden could be viewed from Jacuzzi as well.

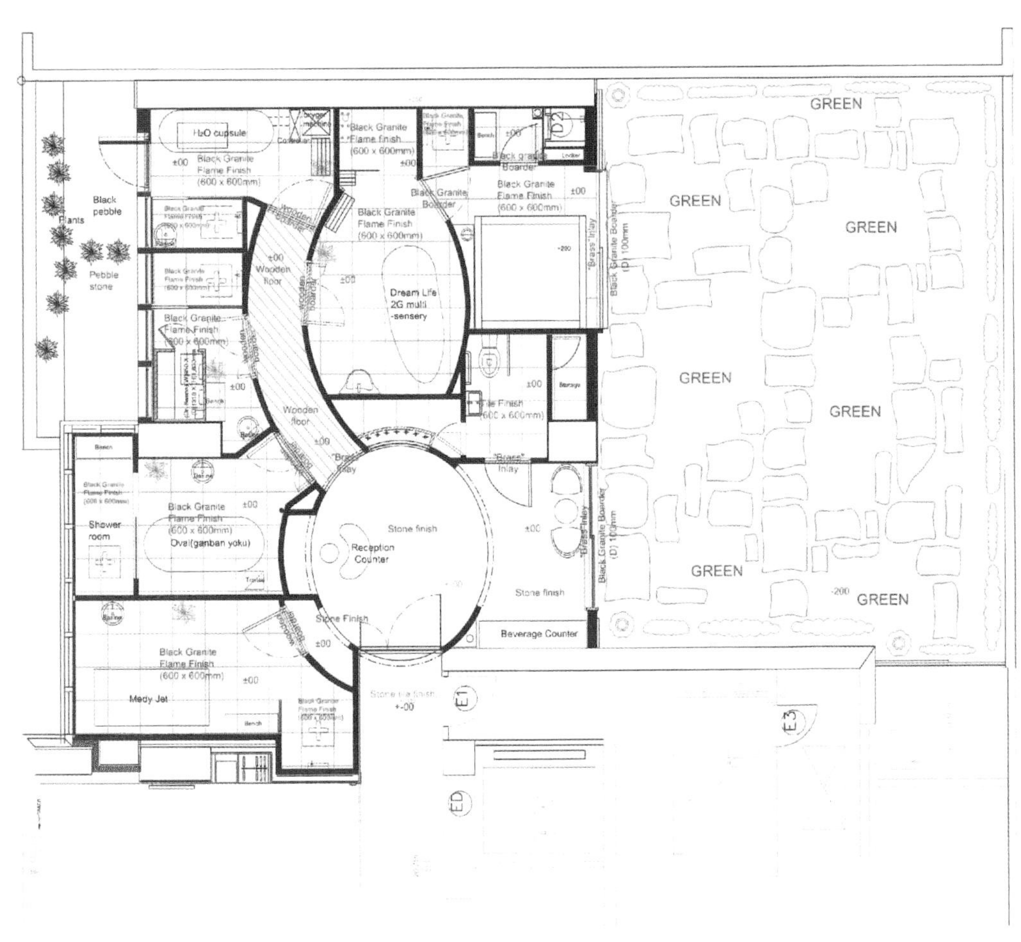

GREEN
GREEN
GREEN
GREEN
GREEN
GREEN
GREEN
H₂O cupsule
Black Granite Flame Finish (600 x 600mm)
Black pebble
Plants
Pebble stone
Wooden floor
Dream Life 2G multi -sensory
Black Granite Boarder
Tile Finish (600 x 600mm)
Brass Inlay
Shower room
Black Granite Flame Finish (600 x 600mm) Oval(ganban yoku)
Stone finish
Reception Counter
Beverage Counter
Medy Jet
Bench
Storage
Locker

ガラス注意
ペアレックス(複層ガラス)
セントラル硝子

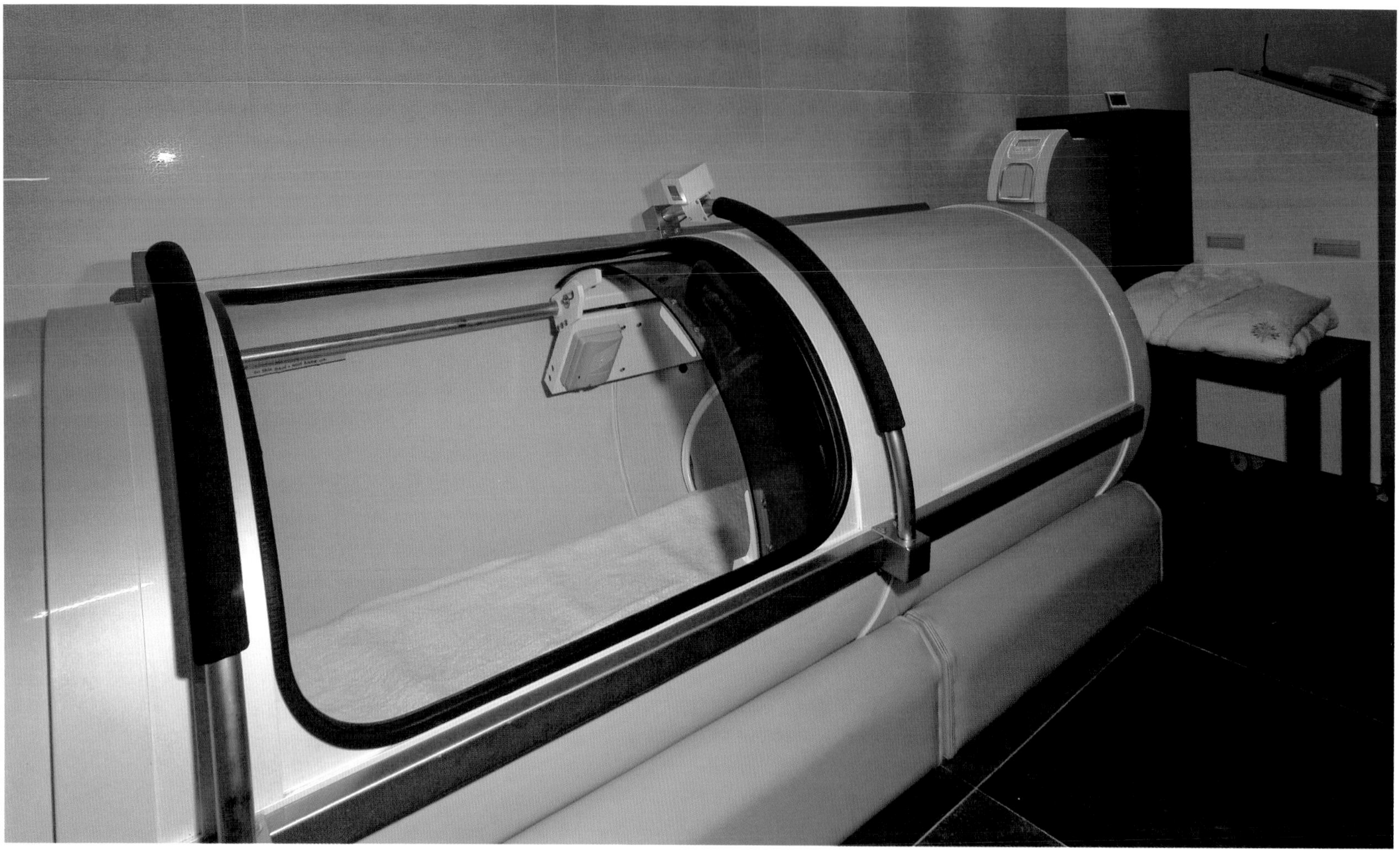

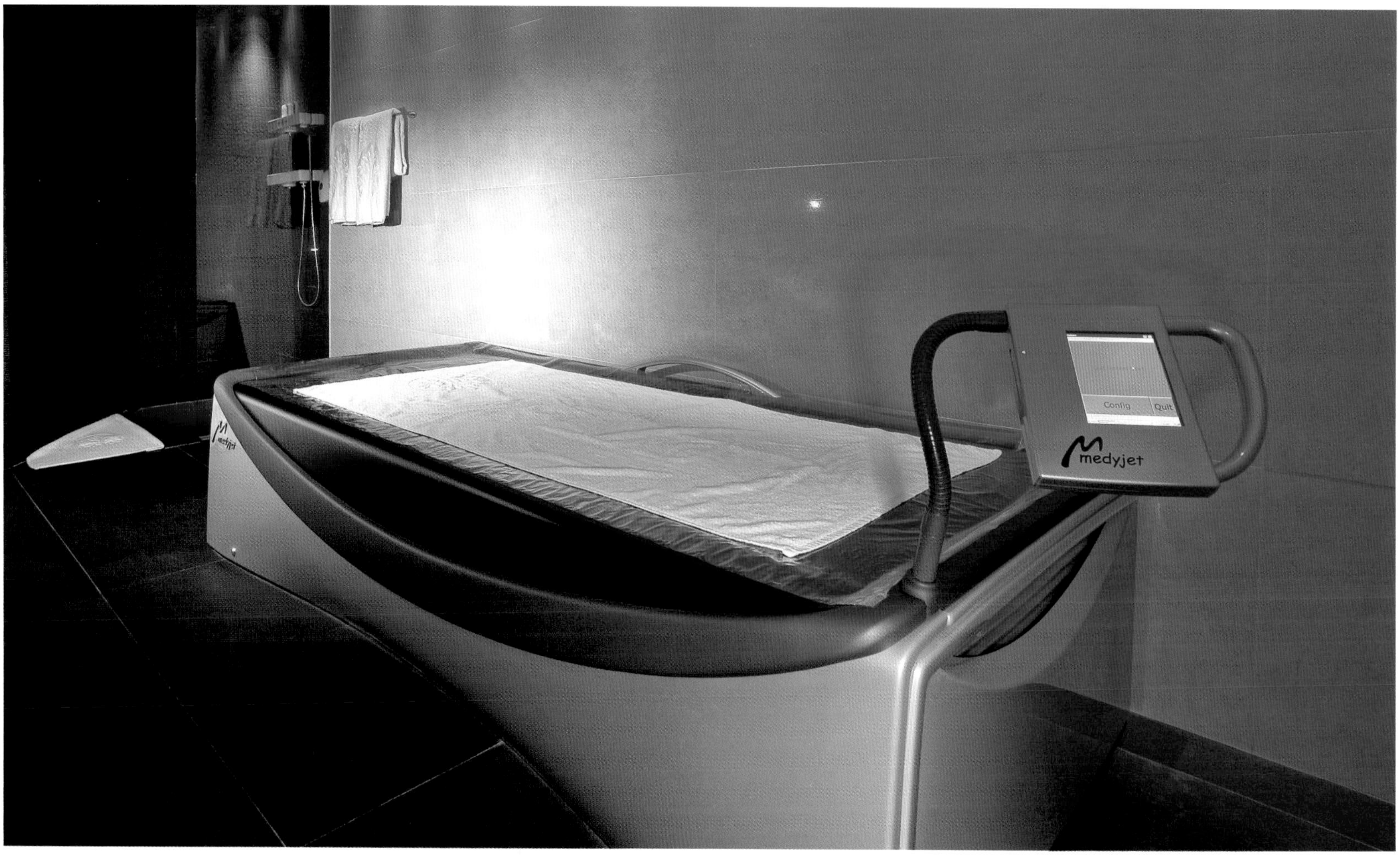

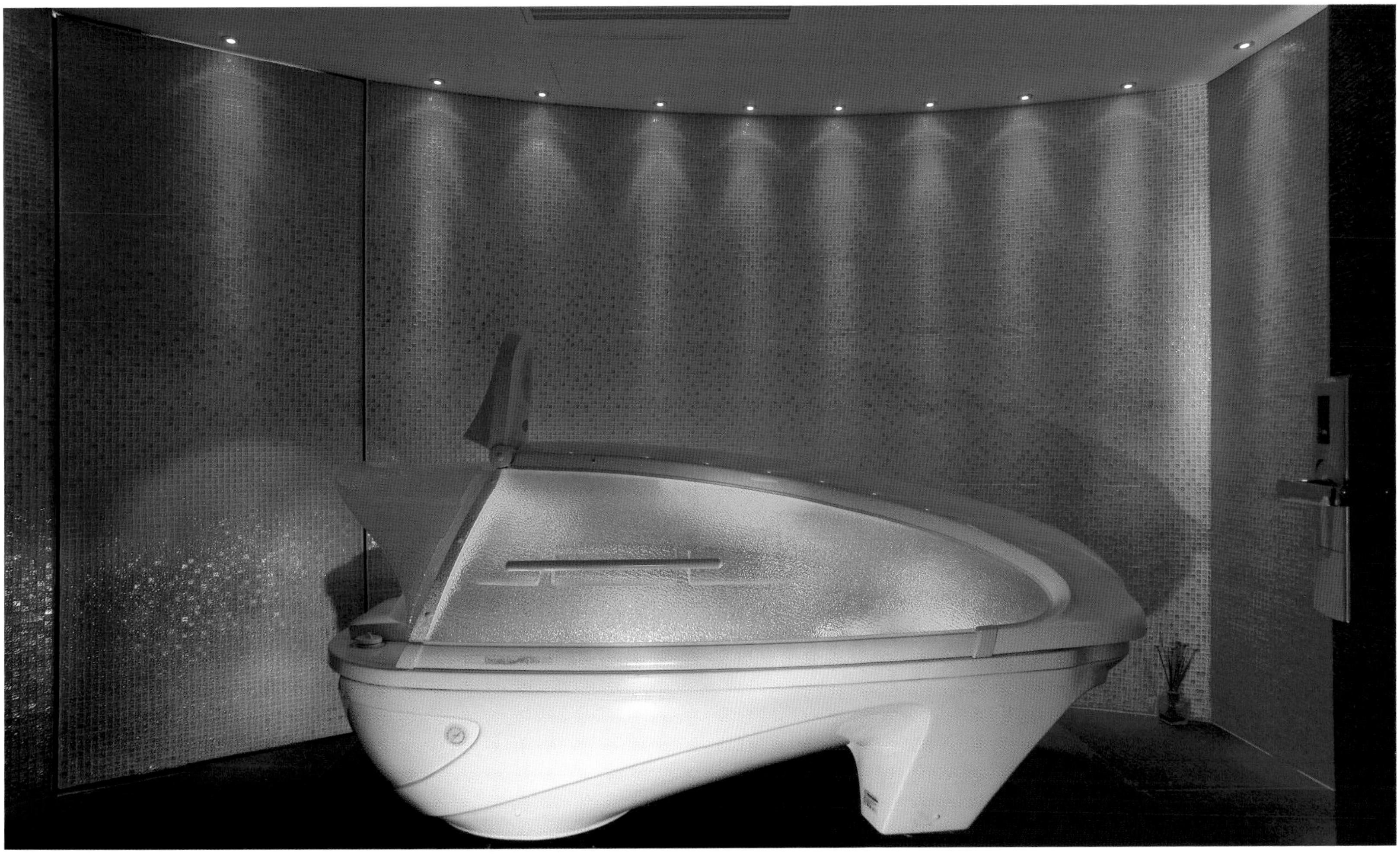

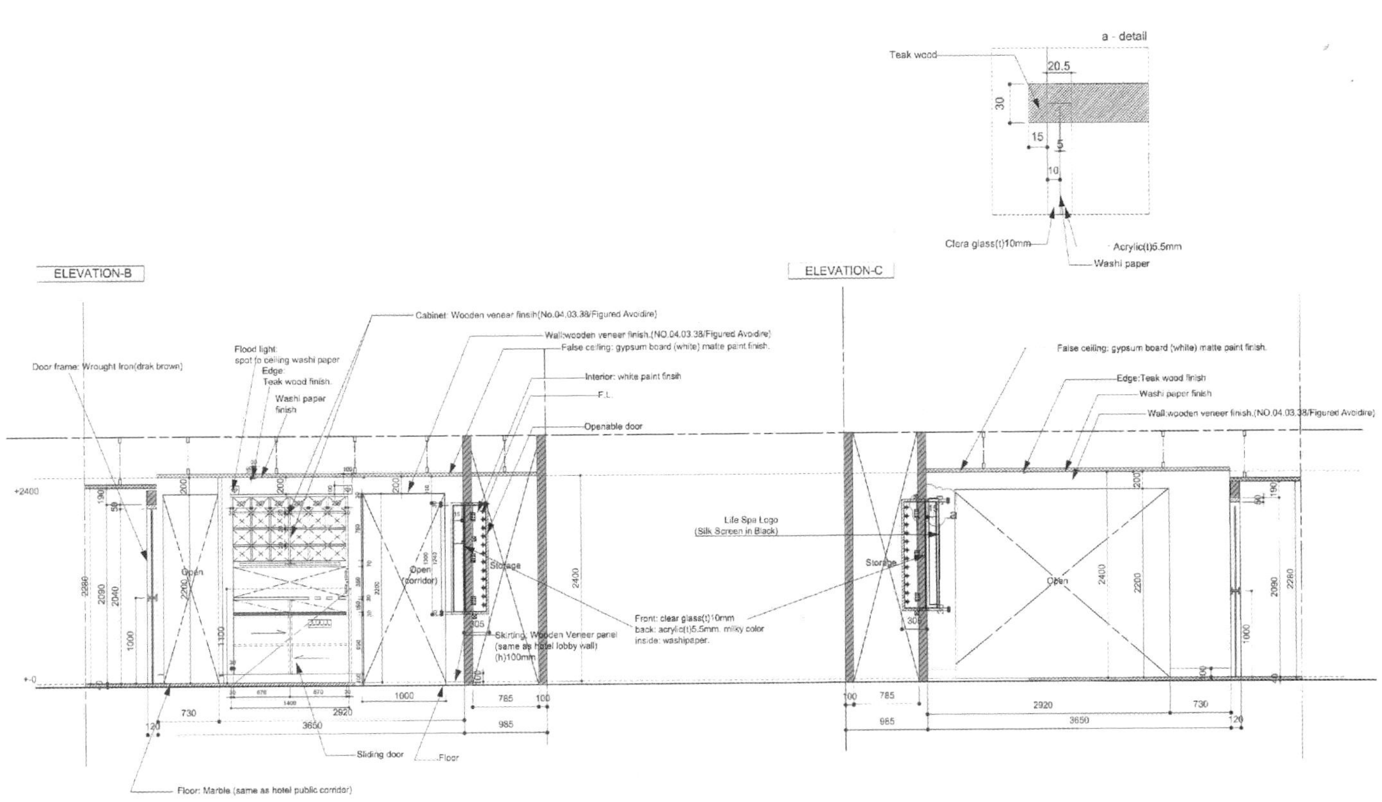
a - detail
Teak wood
20.5
30
15
5
10
Clera glass(t)10mm
Acrylic(t)5.5mm
Washi paper
ELEVATION-B
Cabinet: Wooden veneer finsih(No.04.03.38/Figured Avoidire)
Wall:wooden veneer finish.(NO.04.03.38/Figured Avoidire)
False ceiling: gypsum board (white) matte paint finish.
Flood light:
spot to ceiling washi paper
Edge:
Teak wood finish.
Washi paper
finish
Door frame: Wrought Iron(drak brown)
Interior: white paint finsih
F.L.
Openable door
Open
Open
(corridor)
Storage
Life Spa Logo
(Silk Screen in Black)
Front: clear glass(t)10mm
back: acrylic(t)5.5mm. milky color
inside: washipaper.
Skirting: Wooden Veneer panel
(same as hotel lobby wall)
(h)100mm
Sliding door
Floor
Floor: Marble (same as hotel public corridor)
ELEVATION-C
False ceiling: gypsum board (white) matte paint finish.
Edge:Teak wood finish
Washi paper finish
Wall:wooden veneer finish.(NO.04.03.38/Figured Avoidire)
Storage
Open

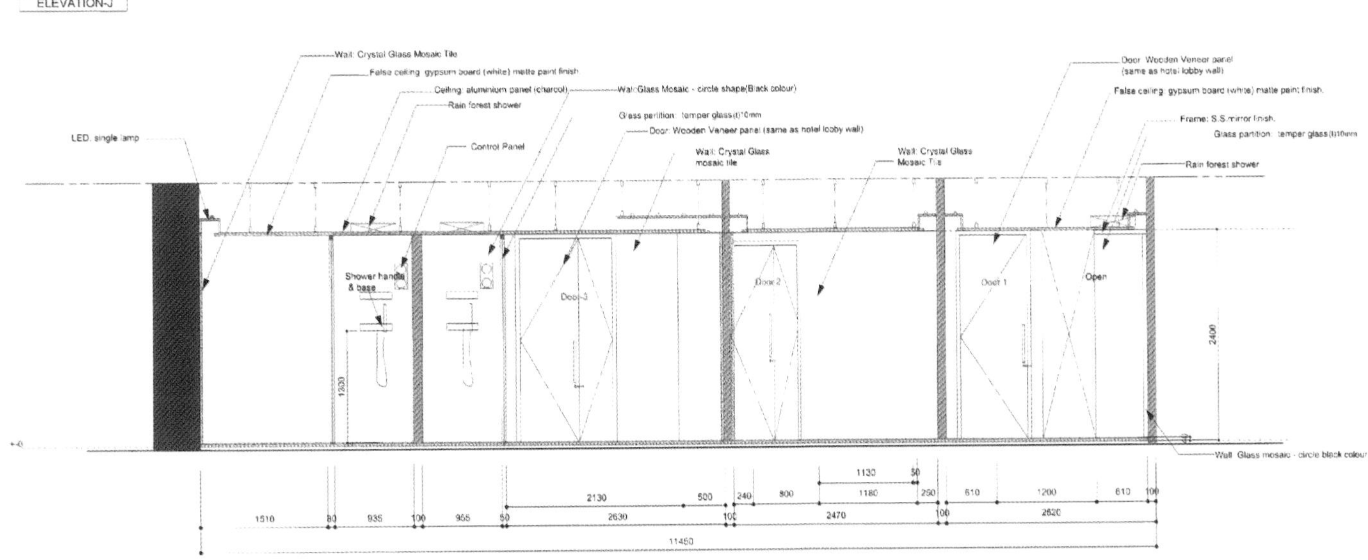
ELEVATION-J
Wall: Crystal Glass Mosaic Tile
False ceiling: gypsum board (white) matte paint finish
Ceiling: aluminium panel (charcol)
Wall:Glass Mosaic - circle shape(Black colour)
Rain forest shower
Glass partition: temper glass(t)10mm
Door: Wooden Veneer panel (same as hotel lobby wall)
LED. single lamp
Control Panel
Wall: Crystal Glass
mosaic tile
Wall: Crystal Glass
Mosaic Tile
Door: Wooden Veneer panel
(same as hotel lobby wall)
False ceiling: gypsum board (white) matte paint finish.
Frame: S.S.mirror finish.
Glass partition: temper glass(t)10mm
Rain forest shower
Shower handle
& base
Door-3
Door 2
Door 1
Open
Wall: Glass mosaic - circle black colour

ESPA at Yas Viceroy Abu Dhabi

VICEROY

Design Agency: Richardson Sadeki
Location: Abu Dhabi

Enter a sanctuary of award-winning rejuvenation at ESPA at Yas Viceroy Abu Dhabi, where classic healing traditions blend with modern techniques to provide an inspirational experience.

ESPA at Yas Viceroy Abu Dhabi transcends the expected, with nine treatment rooms, separate private areas for male and female guests, Kinesis fitness equipment, a relaxation lounge overlooking the Yas Marina race track, plus the Viceroy Presidential Treatment Suite featuring its own hammam steam room with a rain shower and color therapy. Through a detailed offering of spa treatments, each guest will find a tranquil retreat for pampering and relaxation, emerging with a renewed energy and spirit."

ESPA

Pool and Spa area for a Hotel in Mallorca

A2arquitectos

Designer: Juan Manzanares Suarez & Cristian Santandreu Utermark
Client: Hotel Castell dels Hams
Location: Mallorca, Spain
Area: 690 m^2
Photography: Laura Torres Roa y Toni Amengual

The work centered on replacing the covering and enclosure of the existing heated pool and to create an adjacent spa to supplement it.

The pool was originally connected to what was once considered the back of the hotel, where it was confined to a space that was clearly being wasted. The challenge of the project was not only to stop the new areas from being used as secondary features, but to ensure they were used to highlight the hotel's sunniest facade. Now completed, the roof is dotted with windows. This interplay of window holes in the roof creates a beautiful dance of light reflections inside the existing pool has got new facades and a new green roof, which is dotted with a series of square openings. This interplay of window holes creates a beautiful dance of light reflections in the building.

In the spa area, the space is sculpted and colourful showers of light flow through the openings in the roof. This makes the building itself part of the treatment, offering the feeling of well-being created by nature when it is introduced into the building, a feeling of total immersion for the visitor.

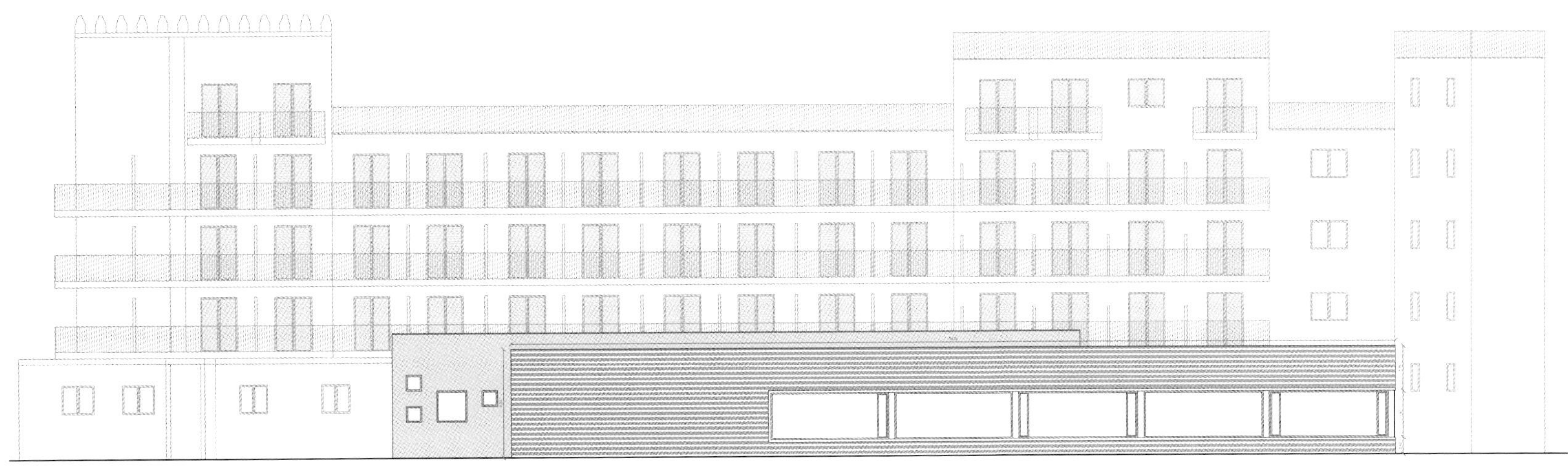

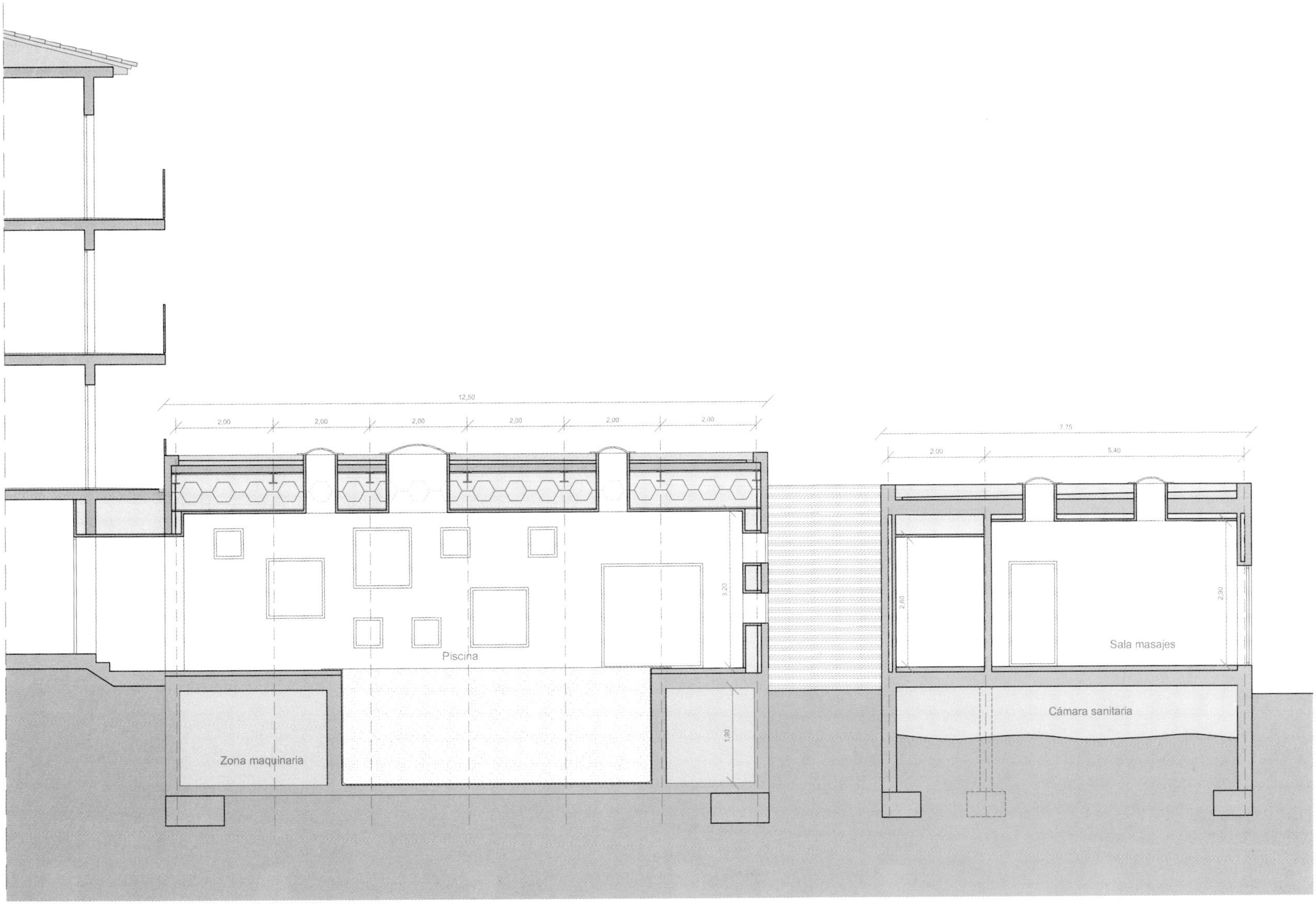

12,50

2,00 2,00 2,00 2,00 2,00 2,00

7,75

2,00 5,40

3,20

2,60

2,90

Piscina

Sala masajes

1,90

Cámara sanitaria

Zona maquinaria

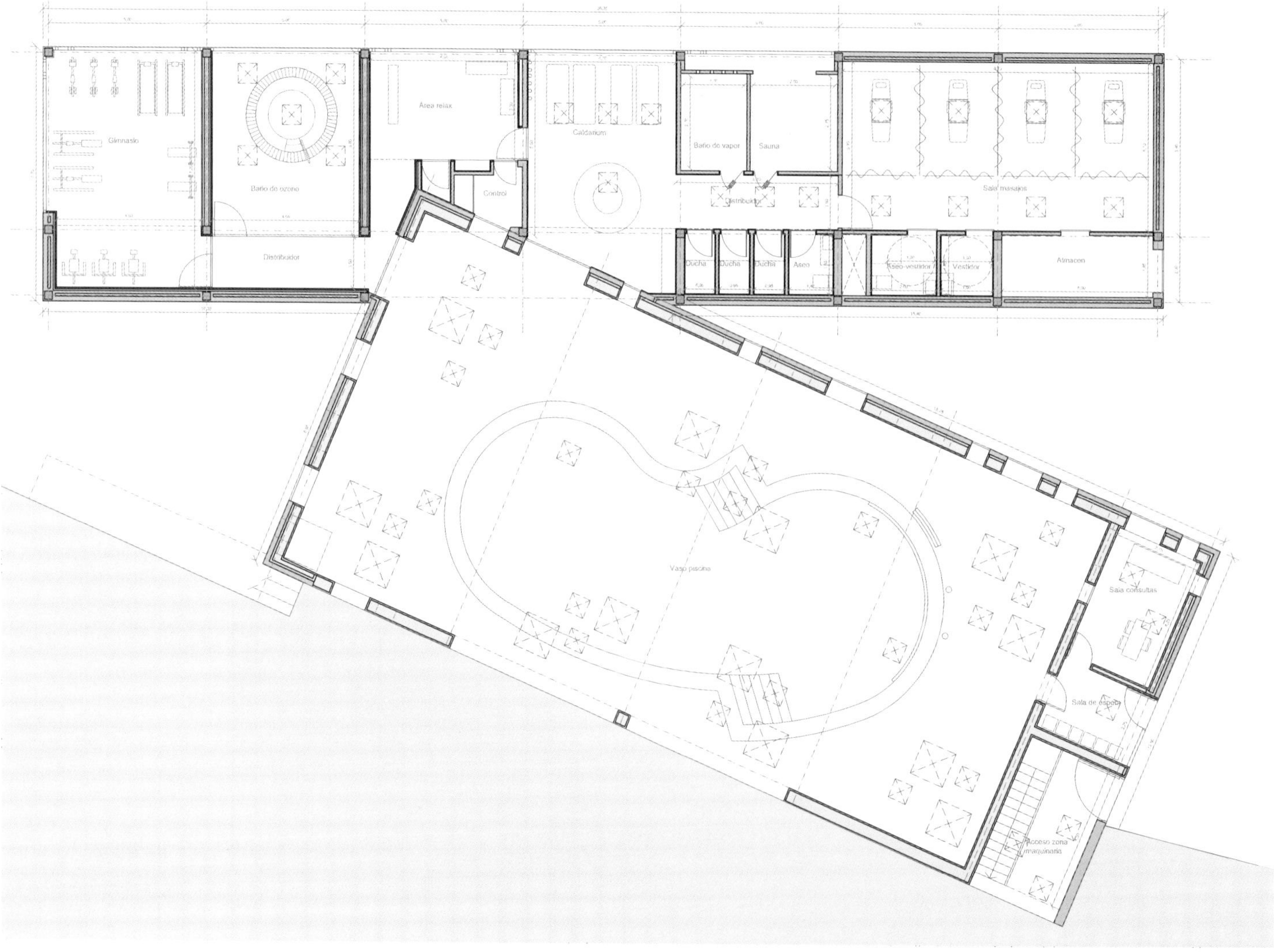

CALDARIUM
T.H.=(30°C~31°C)
HAMA

RELAX

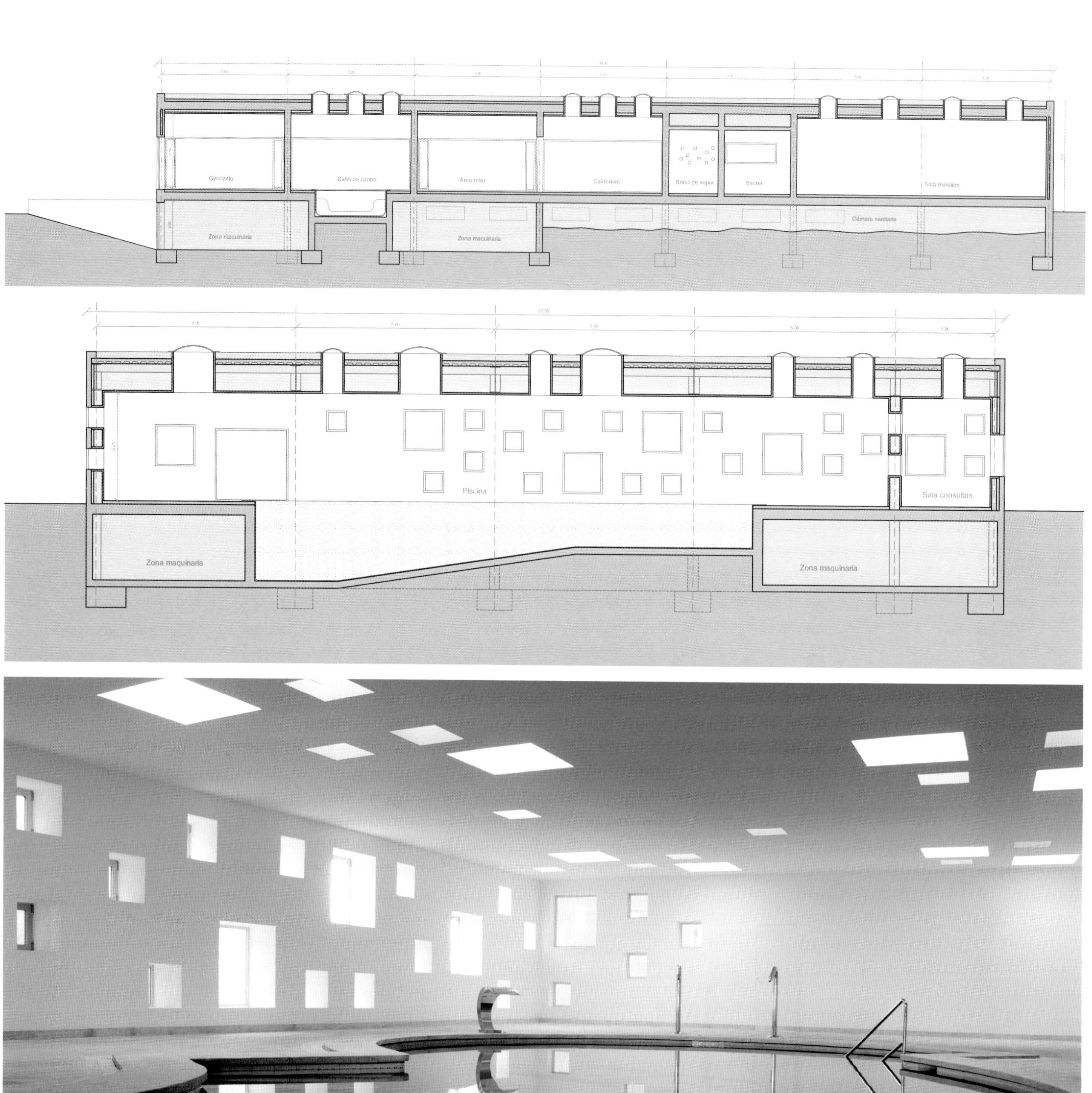
Gimnasio
Baño de ozono
Área relax
Caldarium
Baño de vapor
Sauna
Sala masajes
Cámara sanitaria
Zona maquinaria
Zona maquinaria
Piscina
Sala consultas
Zona maquinaria
Zona maquinaria

Sukhothai Spa Botanica

dwp

Location: Bangkok, Thailand
Area: 350 m²

The Sukhothai Spa Botanica, designed by world-class architecture and interior design firm dwp, evokes serenity and contemporary Thai elegance. The spa is 350sqm, including seven treatment rooms: five single treatment rooms and two suites that can accommodate couples.

For the treatment rooms, the design focused on the concept of "relax, indulge, delight", creating an environment, in which the clientele of the spa can experience luxurious pampering.

Interior finishes and furniture use natural materials, including light-coloured teak, local limestone and silk fabrics. Selected Thai antique art pieces accent the spaces, while highlighted decoration of silver and gold gilded objects and subtle patterns achieve an understated, yet opulent, feel.

The resulting effect is that Sukhothai Spa Botanica's signature spa treatments are provided in an uncomplicated, spacious and warm interior scheme, within the surrounding setting of a tranquil, tropical garden villa.

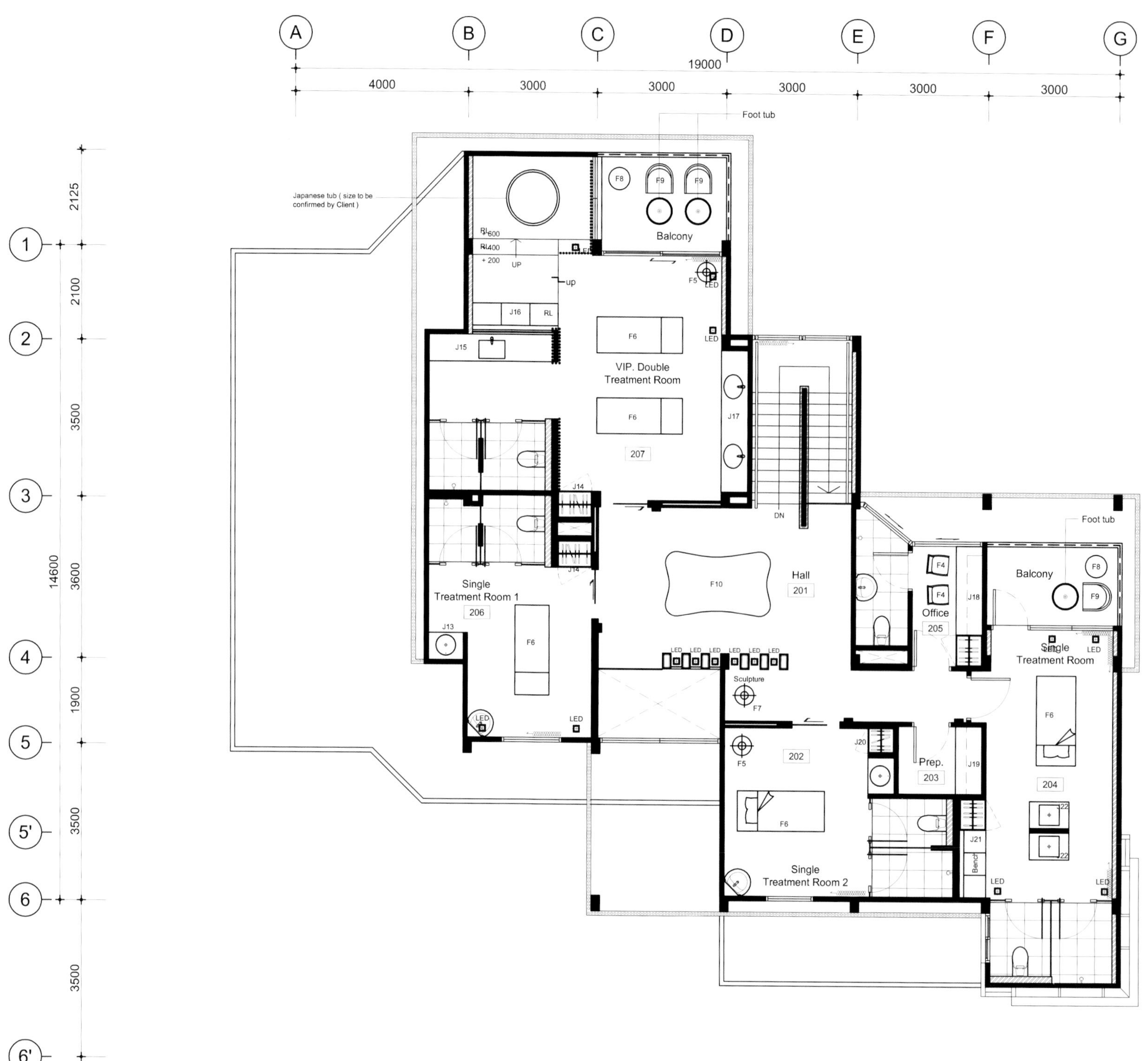

A
B
C
D
E
F
G
19000
4000
3000
3000
3000
3000
3000
Foot tub
Japanese tub (size to be confirmed by Client)
2125
2100
3500
3600
14600
1900
3500
3500
1
2
3
4
5
5'
6
6'
Balcony
VIP. Double Treatment Room
207
Hall
201
Single Treatment Room 1
206
Office
205
Single Treatment Room
204
Prep.
203
202
Single Treatment Room 2
Sculpture
DN
UP
up

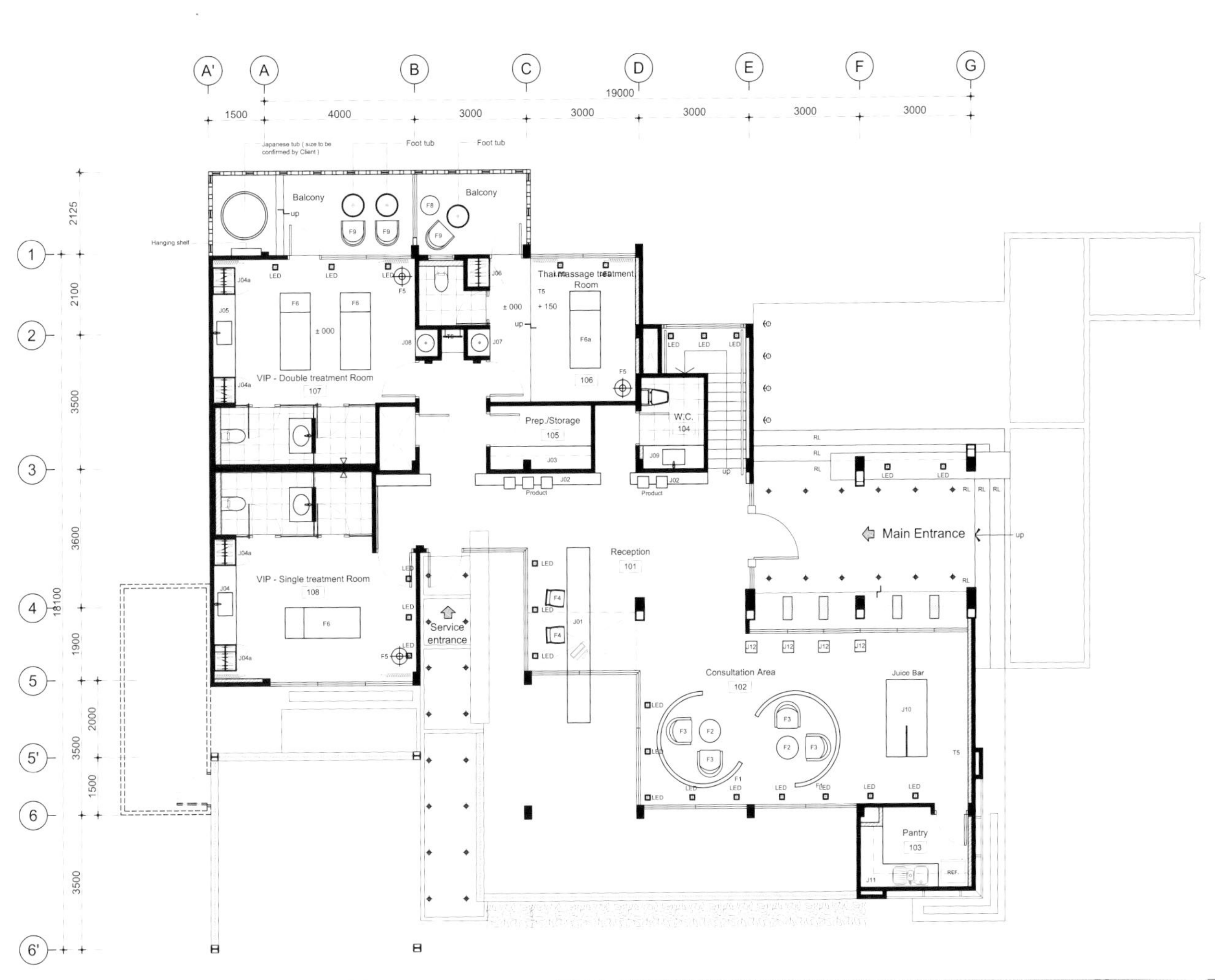

A'
A
B
C
D
E
F
G
19000
1500
4000
3000
3000
3000
3000
3000
Foot tub
Foot tub
Balcony
Balcony
Hanging shelf
Thai massage treatment Room
106
VIP - Double treatment Room
107
Prep./Storage
105
W.C.
104
Product
Product
Main Entrance
VIP - Single treatment Room
108
Service entrance
Reception
101
Consultation Area
102
Juice Bar
Pantry
103
1
2
3
4
5
5'
6
6'
2125
2100
3500
3600
18100
1900
2000
3500
1500
3500

Palazzo Arzaga Spa

Silvia Giannini architetto

Location: Calvagese della Riviera (BS) – Italy
Client: Palazzo Arzaga Hotel SPA & Golf Resort
Area: 500m^2
Photography: Pier Paolo Metelli

Restyling Palazzo Arzaga Spa meant to link the whole complex identity and the new spaces, maintaining the existing spaces, and enriching with new elements. The Spa was in a more modern part of the complex, and had contemporary features even before the restyling: it was important to maintain the elegance of the Palace, excluding a fabrication of history.

Arriving in Arzaga the sensation is to walk in an enchanted park, so the nature was naturally the inspiration element, and flowers are the theme of the project.

All the spaces are sober and elegant; the only decorative element is the flower on each massage room door: enter in Arzaga Spa is like walking in a blooming garden.

The materials selection followed the same concept: traditional materials as marble and mosaic, but performed in a contemporary way.

The Termarium is characterized by the glass mosaic, finding the most precious element in the crocus decoration of the steam door, enhanced inside with mosaic butterflies.

Termarium

The Spa suite, instead, is in traditional yellow marble. Is an exclusive place, with hydro-massage for two persons, exclusive steam and sauna, relaxation area and emotional shower.

Here the idea was to give the sensation of a lounge: the benches of sauna and steam haven't a traditional shape: steam seat here ia a real marble sofa; in the sauna is transformed in a bench with arms... the traditional materials acquire roundness in design.

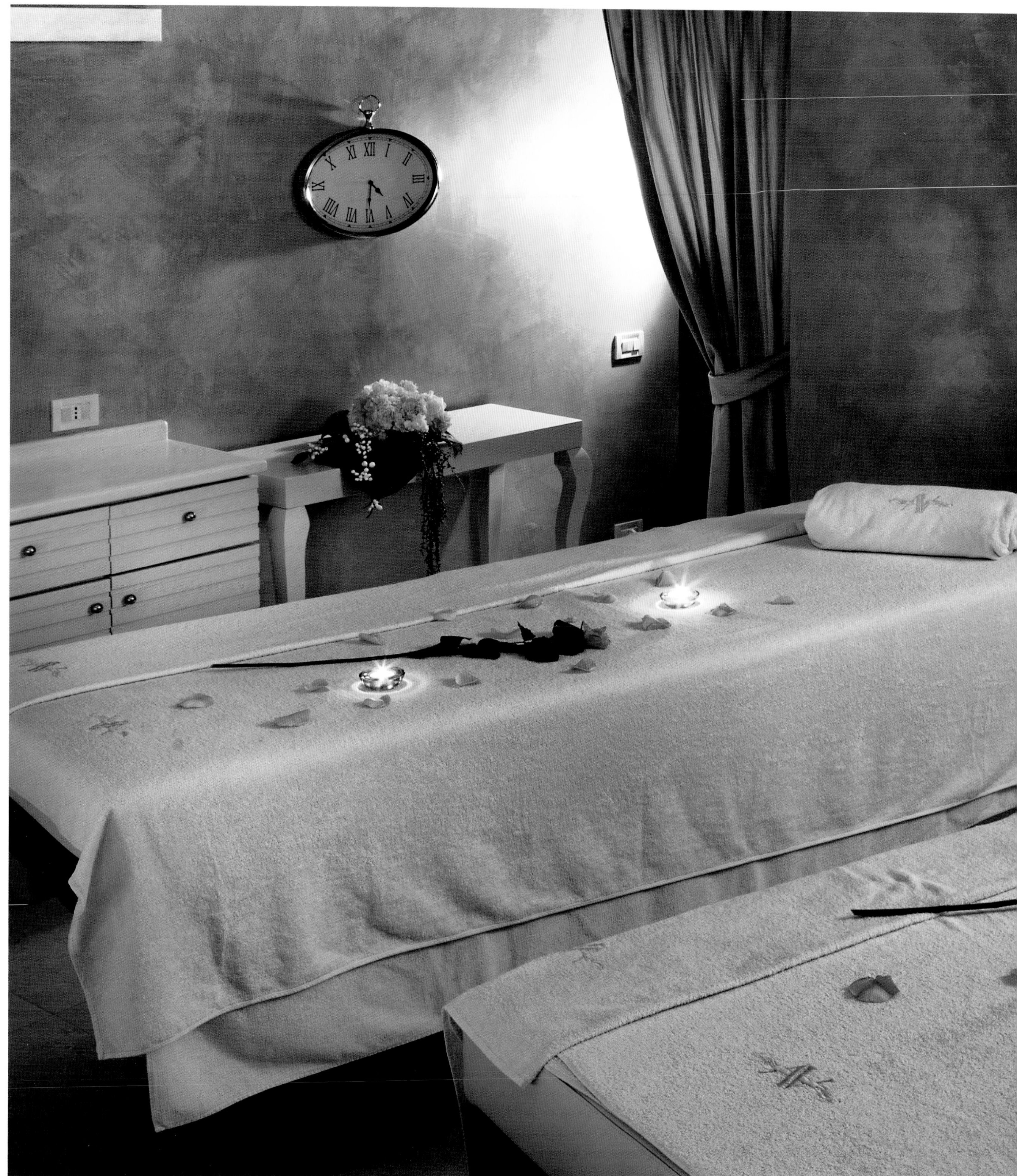

Sihlpark Wellness, Switzerland

Thermarium Baeder-Bau GmbH

Location: Schindellegi, Switzerland
Photography: Markus Auer

Located in Feusisberg, Einsiedeln (30km from Zurich) Sihlpark Wellness is part of a 70.000 m^2 mixed-use real estate development which includes an 82-key four star Ramada hotel. 1590 m^2 spa area with a thermal circuit zone, hamam area, 3 multi-purpose treatment rooms, fitness centre, 1 spa suite as well as a swimming pool. Supporting the overall concept was a compelling mix of amenities and services that were designed to serve both local residents and guests from the adjacent hotel.

The uniquenesss: The self-service hamam. The self-service hamam concept was designed to allow guest to go on the journey themselves and be in complete control of various therapeutic stages of the hamam experience without the need for therapist guidance. This was achieved by user-friendly navigation providing guests with a waterproof map that helped guide them through various hamam thermal rooms and water experiences. The low entry price for the hamam increase also the guest demand and affordability for the rasul bath and soap massage stations located at the end of the hamam journey.

sihlpark
wellness
BIO SAUNA

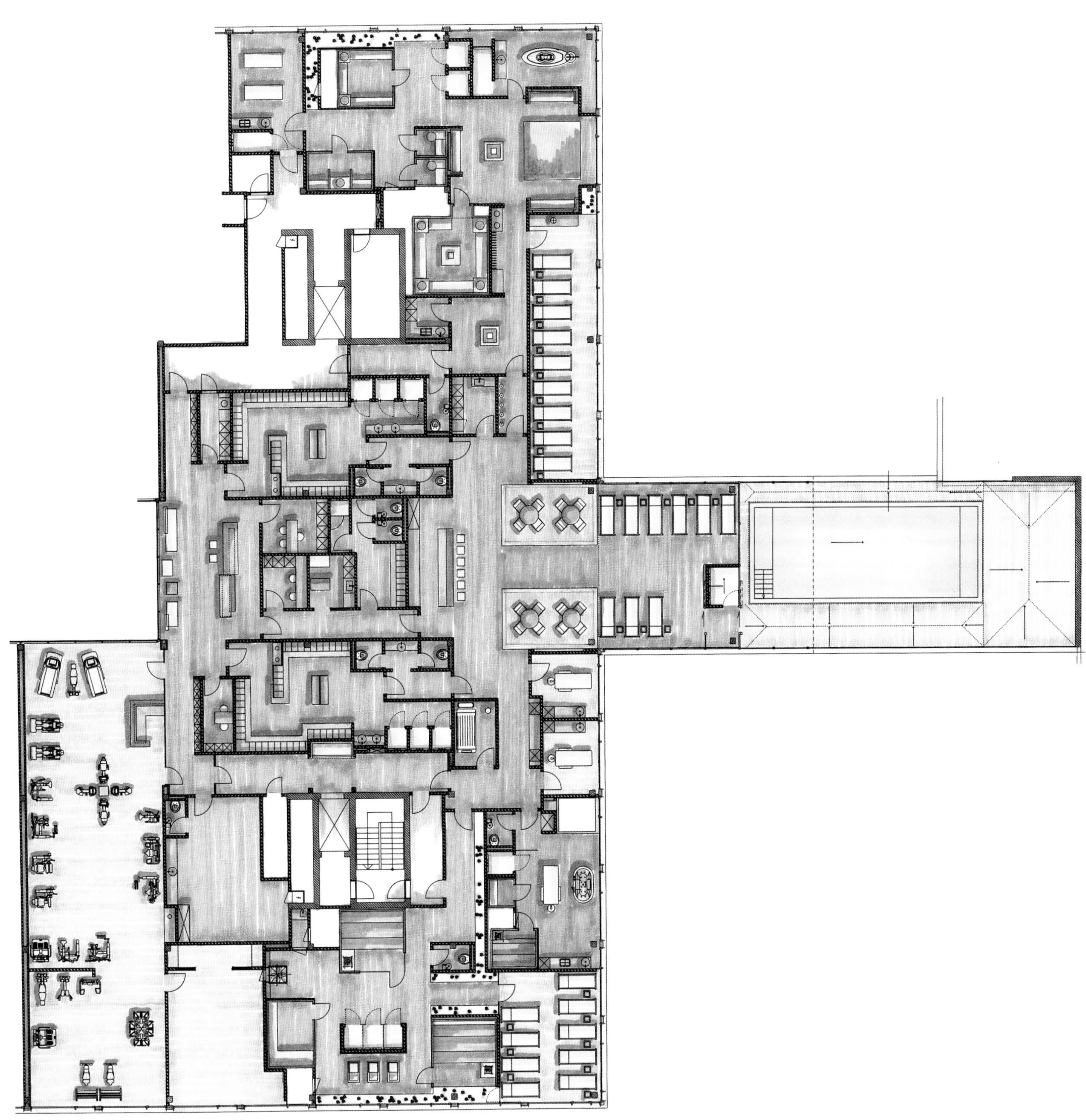

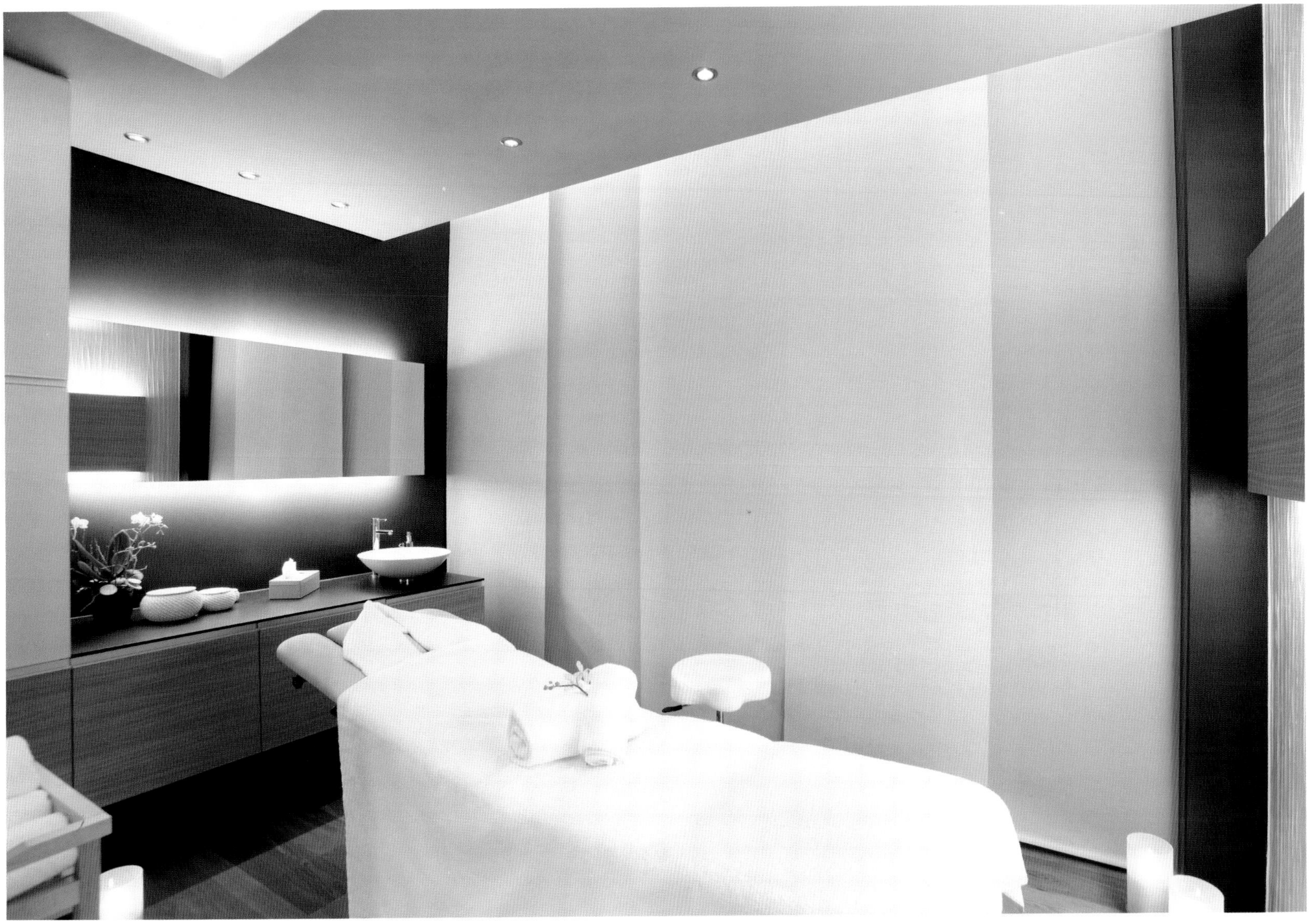

Sheng Ji Yuan Spa

Zhou Shaoyu

Location: Fuzhou, Fujian
Building Area: 275 m^2
Main Materials: Vitrified Tile, Wallpaper, Grey Mirror, Clear Glass

Water is the source of all things. The case has applied the form of water as design element throughout the project. Spectacular waves and beautiful ripples has constituted the vibrant spring and become the main element of the whole space. The case has created tranquil atmosphere through the warm and white tone, with the LED energy-saving lighting system, HIFI surrounding background music system and fresh ventilation and air conditioning system, to provide a fresh, spacious, harmonious, comfortable low-carbon and energy-saving business environment.

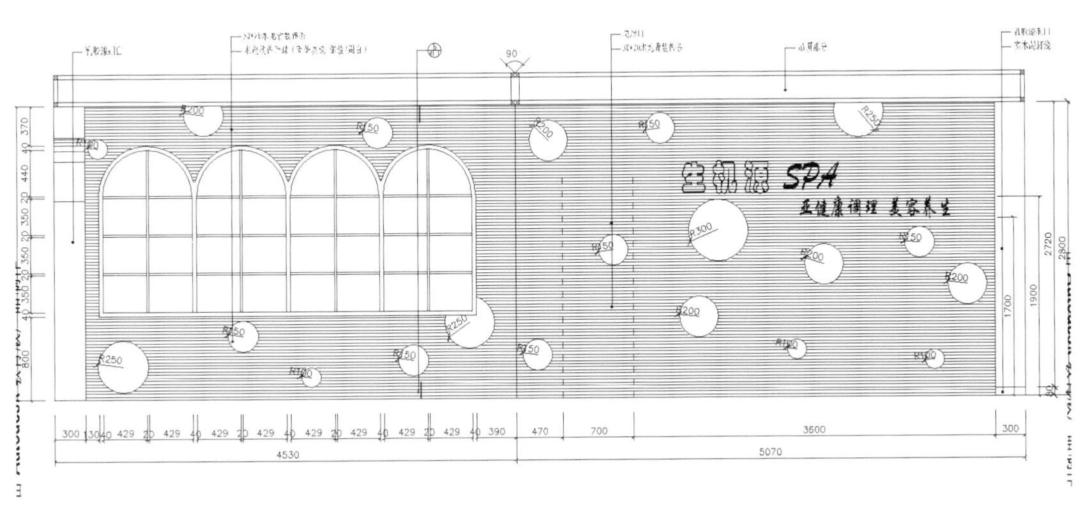
生机源 SPA
亚健康调理 美容养生
R300
R250
R200
R150
300 130 40 429 20 429 40 429 20 429 40 429 20 429 40 429 20 429 40 390
470
700
3600
300
4530
5070
1700
1900
2720
2800

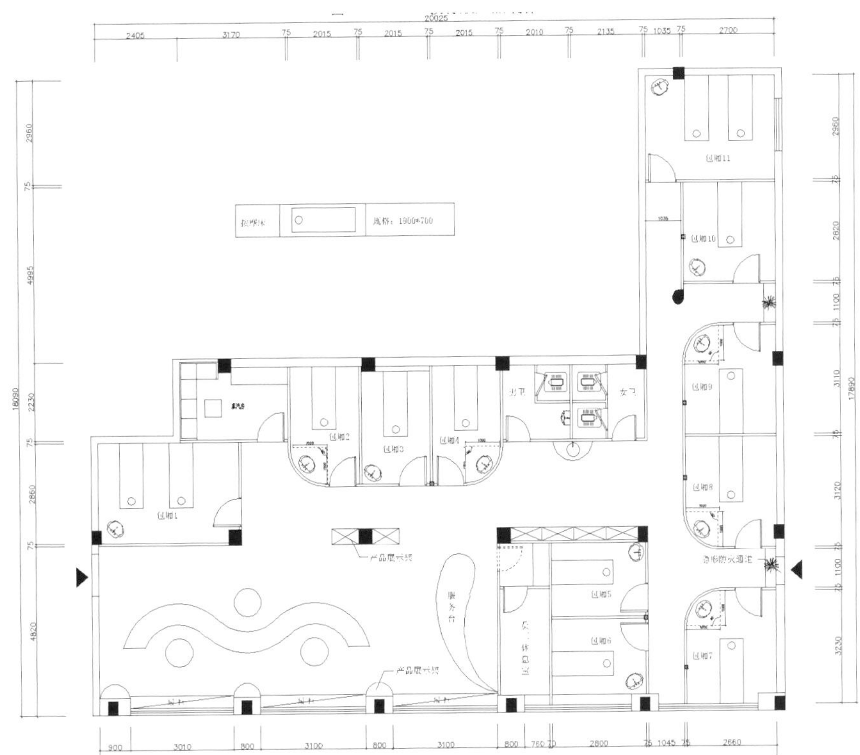

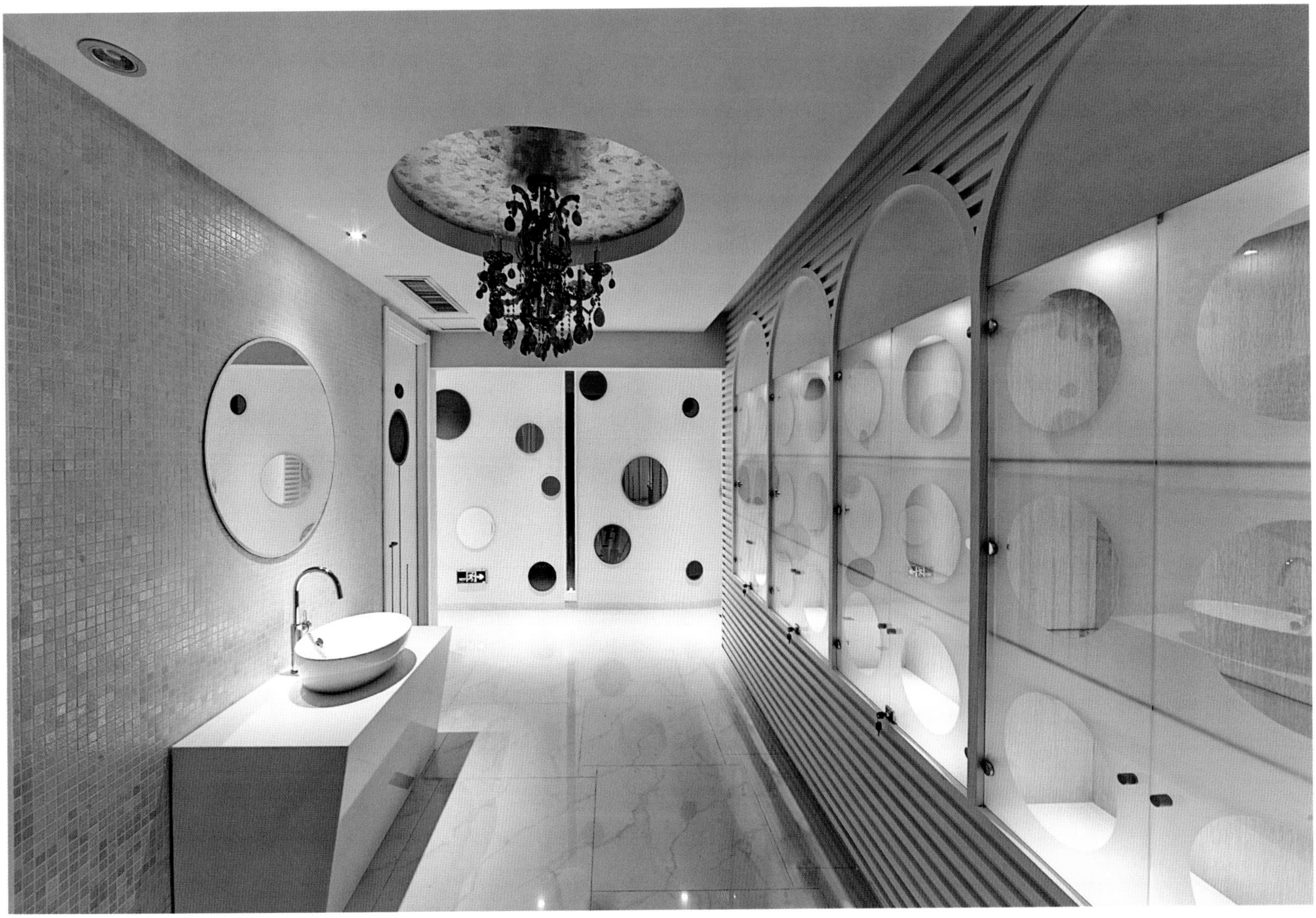

W London Spa

Concrete

Client: McAleer & Rushe Group, Starwood Hotels & Resorts
Location: W hotel London Leicester Square, London, UK
Photography: Ewout Huibers

Guests who need a little extra relaxation can enjoy it at the Away Spa. Curtains of white and silver strings make a delicate entrance to the reception desk, where you can book a massage or a visit to the sauna or steam bath. Before or in between the treatments you can relax on bespoke sofas in the middle of the spa. The five treatment rooms have white leather daybeds and recessed high gloss white laminate walls with LED lighting to support any required mood. When a room is in use, the walls can be closed. When a treatment room is open (not in use), the round corners of the central relax area extend into the treatment room and create a different sense of space. Both the sauna (white space) and the steam room (black space) can be found behind the red glass doors. The red glass points out that you're entering a hot-zone. Three unisex cubicles combine shower, toilets and changing facilities.

REN

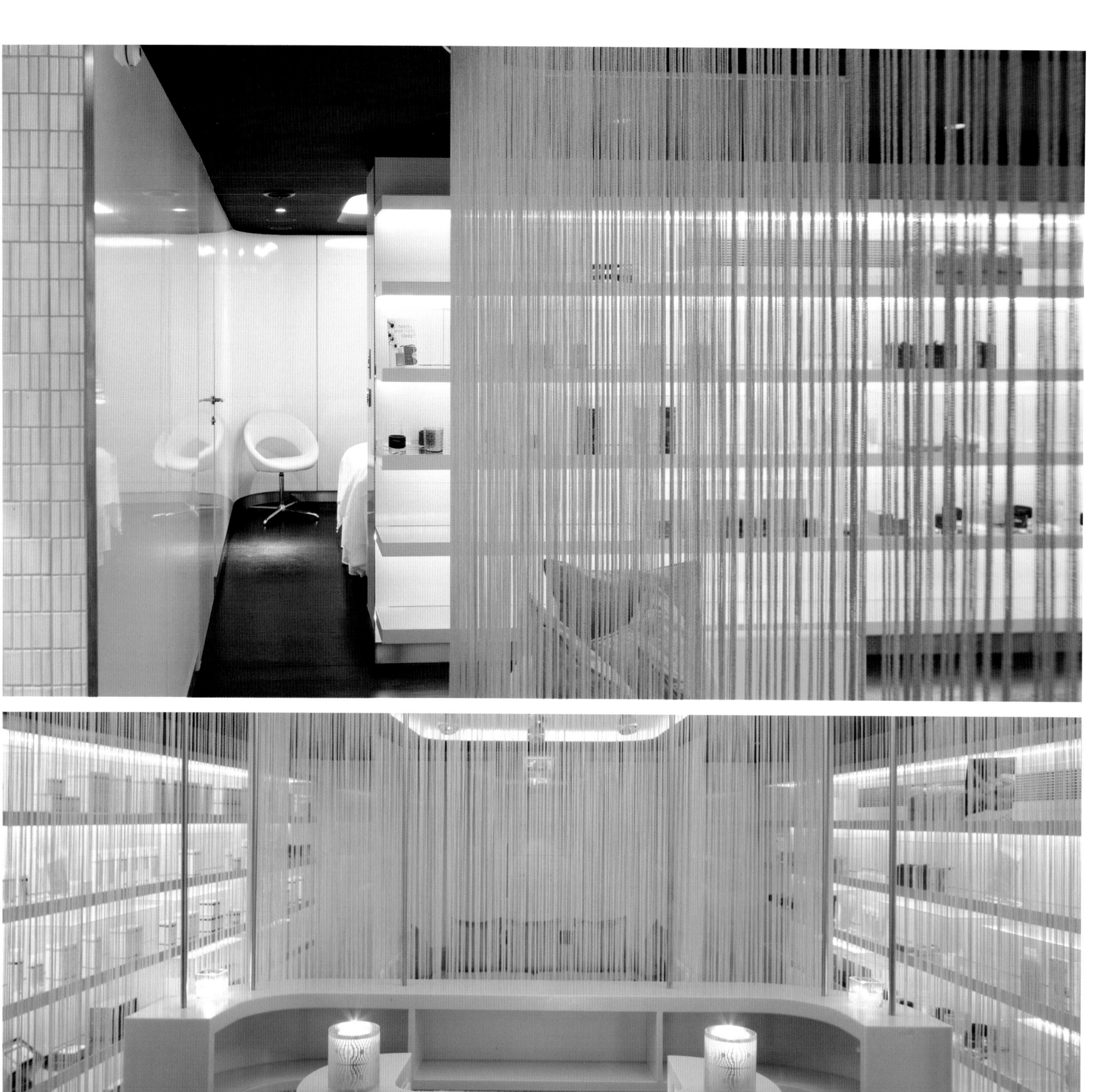

Spa Calme

Igloodgn

Client: Miss Bexon
Location: Montreal, Canada
Area: 232.258 m^2
Year: 2012

The Spa Calme motto is "always anticipate your client's needs", and this quaint-stylish and relaxing destination does just that. Their dominating strength is a cutting edge expertise with a very clear understanding of the clients' needs.

To create an interior design and brand identity to promote the spa as the local 'Spa Authority' while increasing sales through the greater interaction with the qualified estheticians.

Igloodgn created a brand culture and spa design that helped to break down the emotional and physical barriers between customers and estheticians by utilizing a sophisticated - yet unpretentious environmental design.

The spa interior design and brand culture has been a success. The space is not only functional, but it is extremely refined without being intimidating.

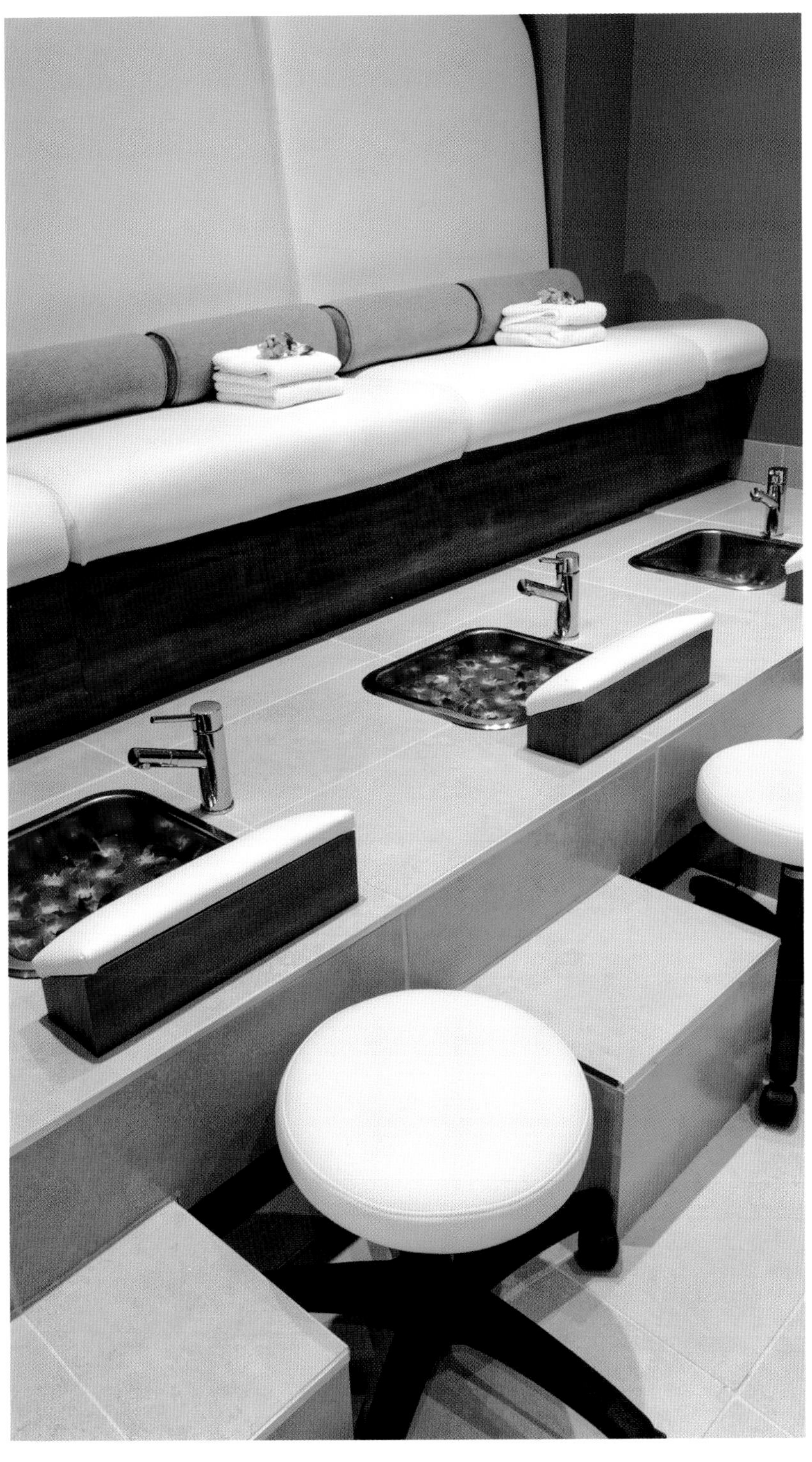

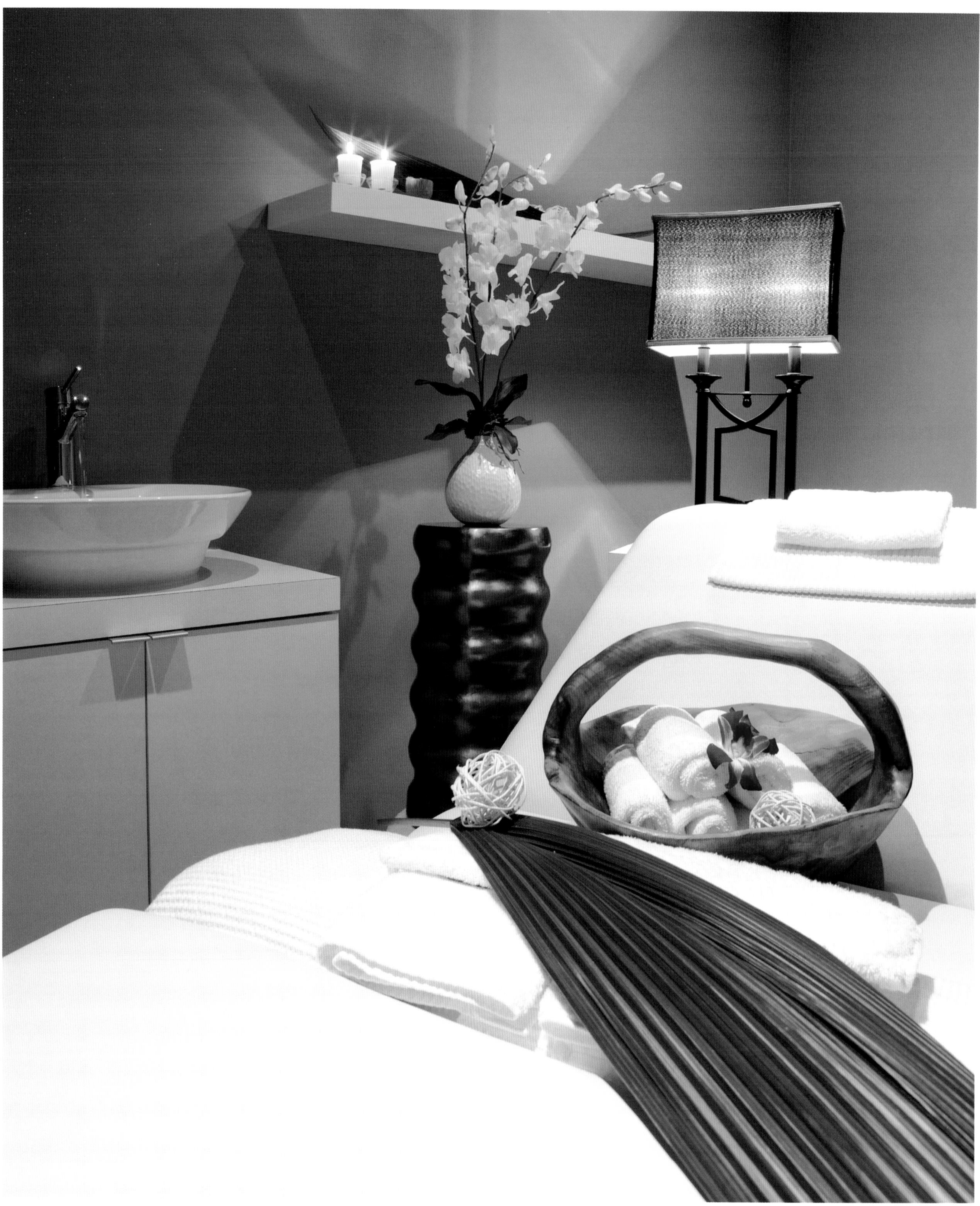

Musica

De Jorio Design International

The project Musica spa has a unique Italian style, which manifests elegance, comfort and luxury. We have designed the interior in an artistic way, to ensure that every room is memorable.

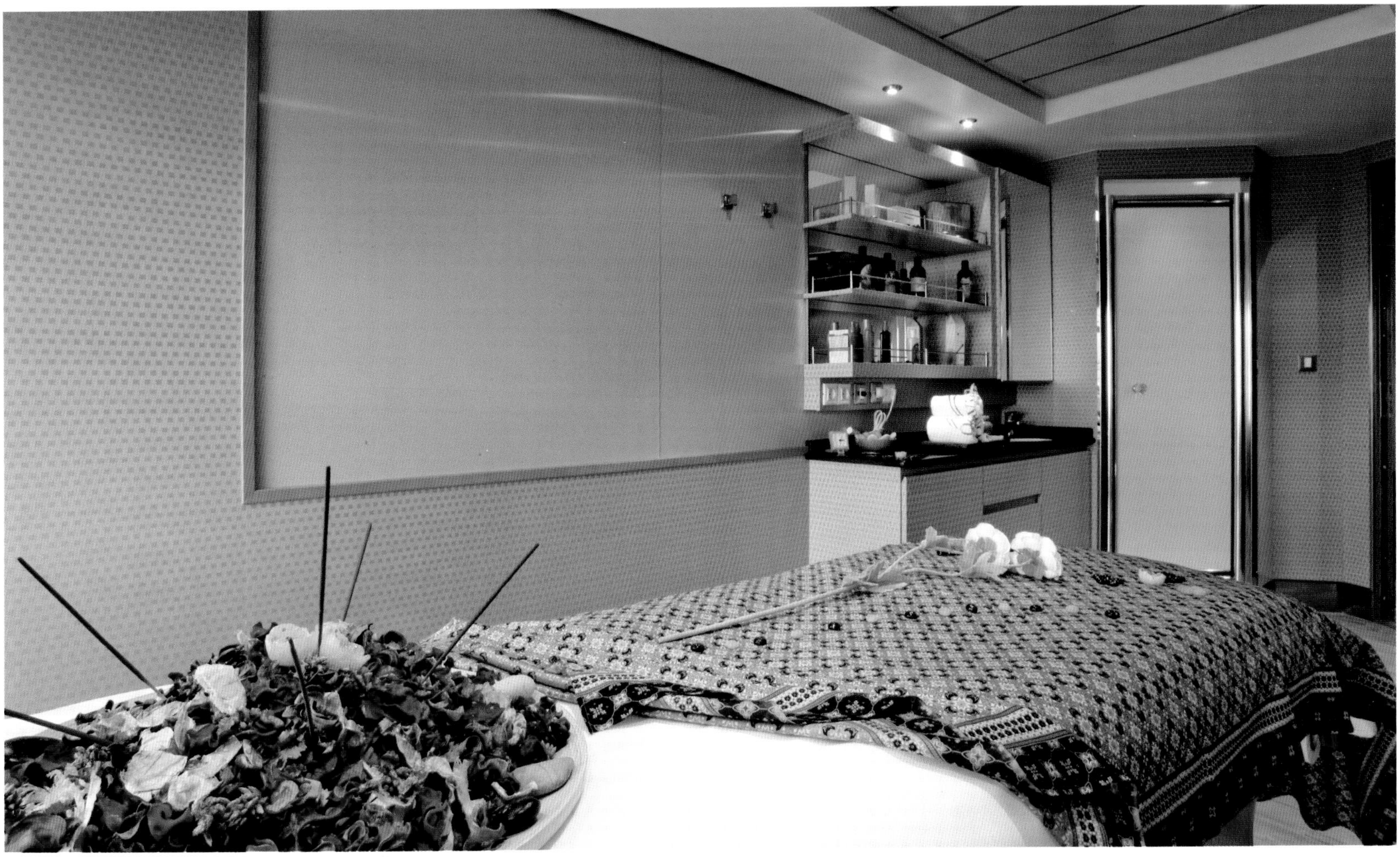

Hotel Massage Room

JOSIF MILENKOVIC

The interior of four massage rooms is a part of a large project of hotel spa center interior. The wish of the investor was to adopt Bali style throughout the center. Psychology of clients was largely considered while creating space. Although these rooms follow the general idea of Bali style (mainly in use of bamboo trees and some decorative details), they differ from other rooms by the degree of oriental geometric elements. The circular forms are dominant in two of four rooms and they have played the key role in endowing visual authenticity to the space. They appear in the arch shaped door frame between two massage rooms, and also as mirror frame in one room and frame of the lighting in the other. Doors that separate the rooms are made of semitransparent wooden material so the rooms visually correspond with each other. This also creates a felling of a larger space, but without disturbing much-needed privacy. Majority of the materials are natural, and the predominant color scheme is earthy colors of similar tones. Tonality contrasts were deliberately reduced to a minimum, since the purpose of the massage rooms is to create an atmosphere that relaxes the body and calms the mind. The lighting comes from different sources, and gives the user variety of options for adapting atmosphere of the room according to wishes and needs of a client. It is meagerly diffuse or ambient which contributes to a pleasant feeling of warmth and carefree mood.

SPA 7 Colors

Irina Samoylova

Client: Chain salons 7 colors
Location: Perm, Russia
Photography: Irina Samoylova

The name of this project is "salon of the seven colors". As it is possible to see in the picture, each massage room has a different color that defines the room itself. In particular shower bath identifies the room name as: blue room, red room and so on. This Salon is located on the top floor of a tall office building and before the refurbishment works, which transformed it into a Thai massage center, it was a commercial office.

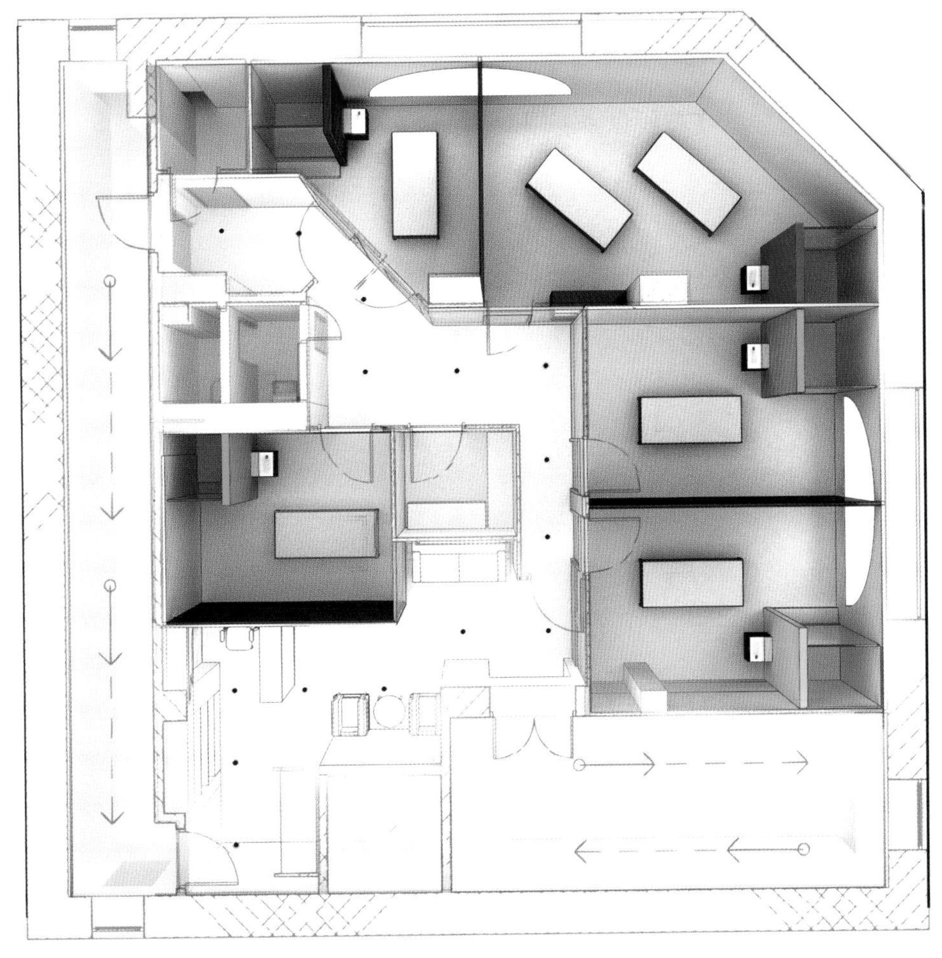

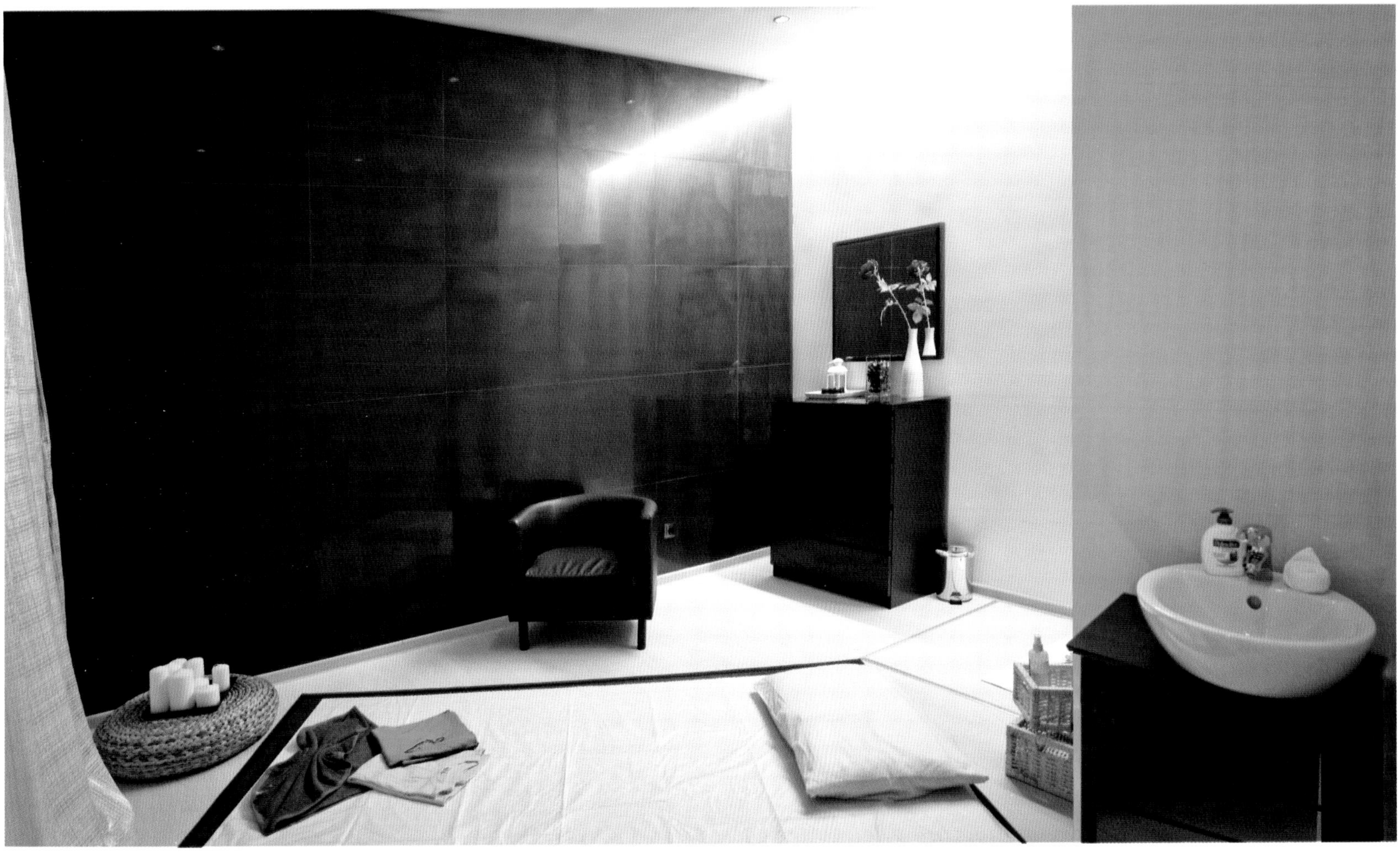

Exhale Mindbody Spa

S3 Design Inc.

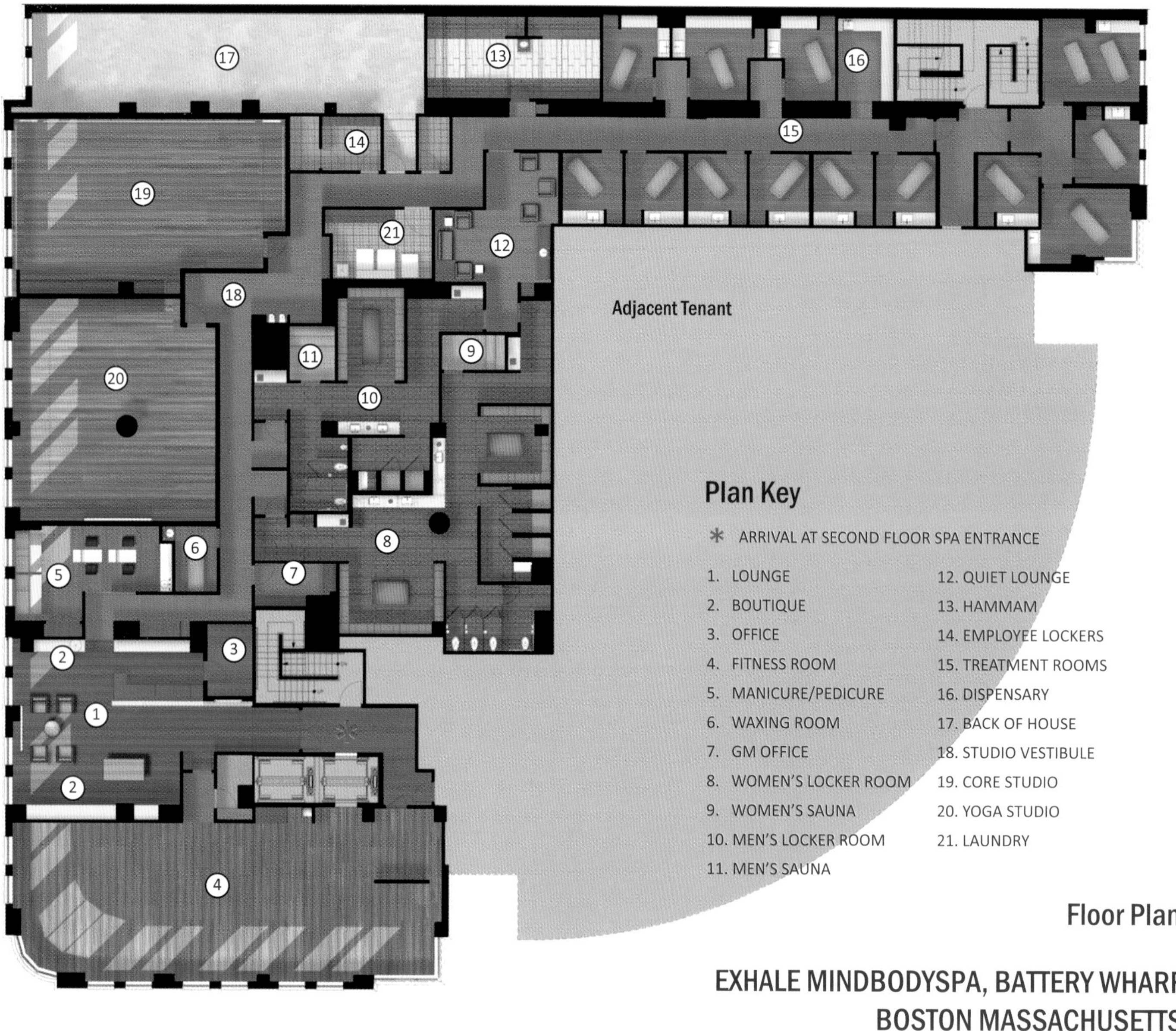

Client: Exhale Enterprises / PNC Bank
Location: 2 Battery Wharf, Boston MA 02109
Area: 1,207.7 m²
Photography: Kristen Teig Photography
Others: DLDT Associates, Legatt McCall Associates

Exhale Mind Body Spas, are the embodiment of holistic spiritual wellbeing, and their flagship location in Boston, is no exception. This location boasts a luxuries locker room and spa, but at the heart of their mission, is the Yoga and Core Studios. The core studio is designed to maximize the proprietary CORE programming, while the Yoga Studio is design to capture the spiritual side of wellbeing. A wooden ceiling trellis is used to hide the minimal lighting that accents the exterior windows. The use of dark woods, rich red drapery, and a rattan woven column enclosure, in the Yoga Studio captures the solemn nature of the yoga experience.

exhale

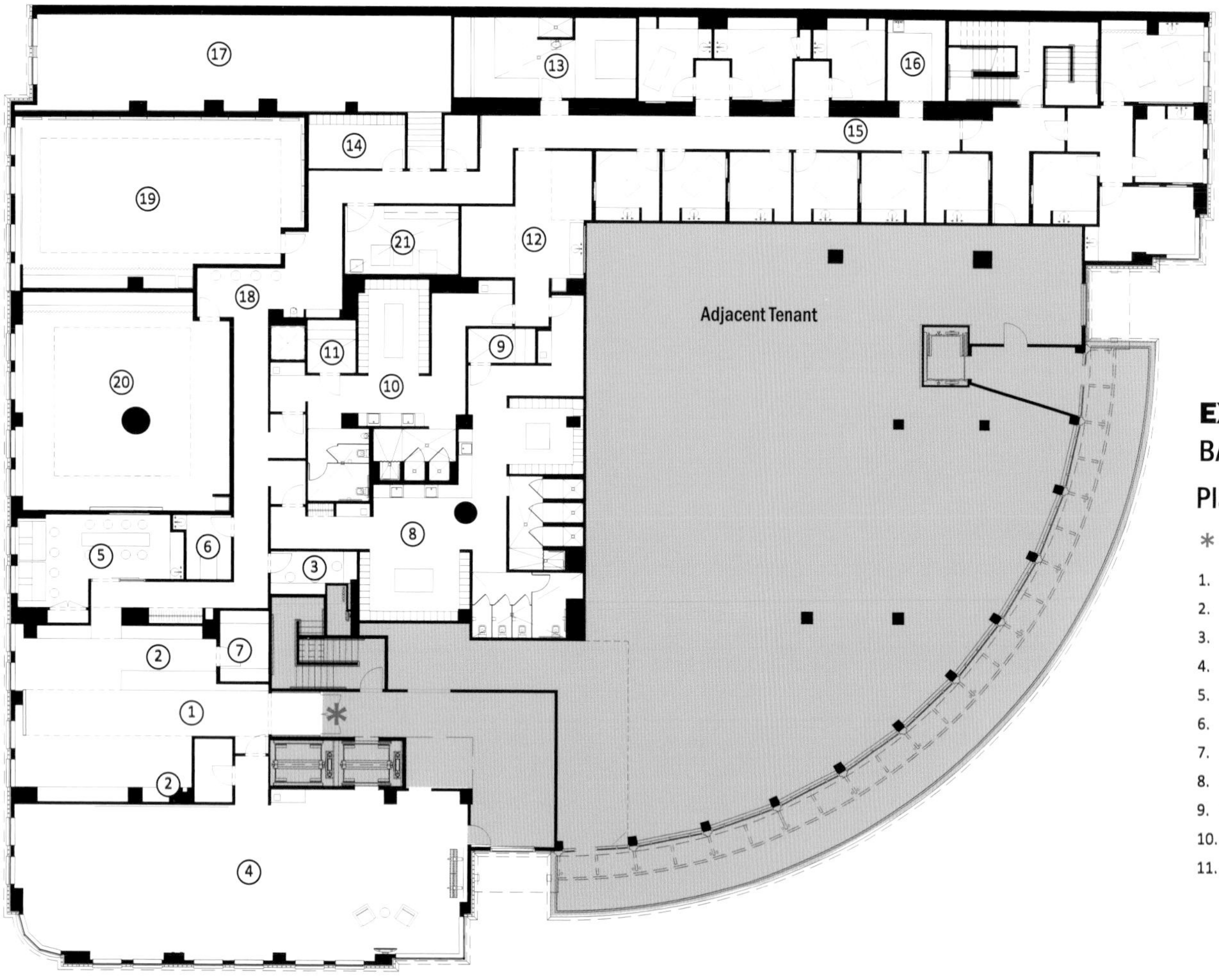

Adjacent Tenant

EXHALE MindBodySpa

BATTERY WHARF BOSTON, MA

Plan Key

* ARRIVAL AT SECOND FLOOR SPA ENTRANCE

1. LOUNGE
2. BOUTIQUE
3. OFFICE
4. FITNESS ROOM
5. MANICURE/PEDICURE
6. WAXING ROOM
7. GM OFFICE
8. WOMEN'S LOCKER ROOM
9. WOMEN'S SAUNA
10. MEN'S LOCKER ROOM
11. MEN'S SAUNA
12. QUIET LOUNGE
13. HAMMAM
14. EMPLOYEE LOCKERS
15. TREATMENT ROOMS
16. DISPENSARY
17. BACK OF HOUSE
18. STUDIO VESTIBULE
19. CORE STUDIO
20. YOGA STUDIO
21. LAUNDRY

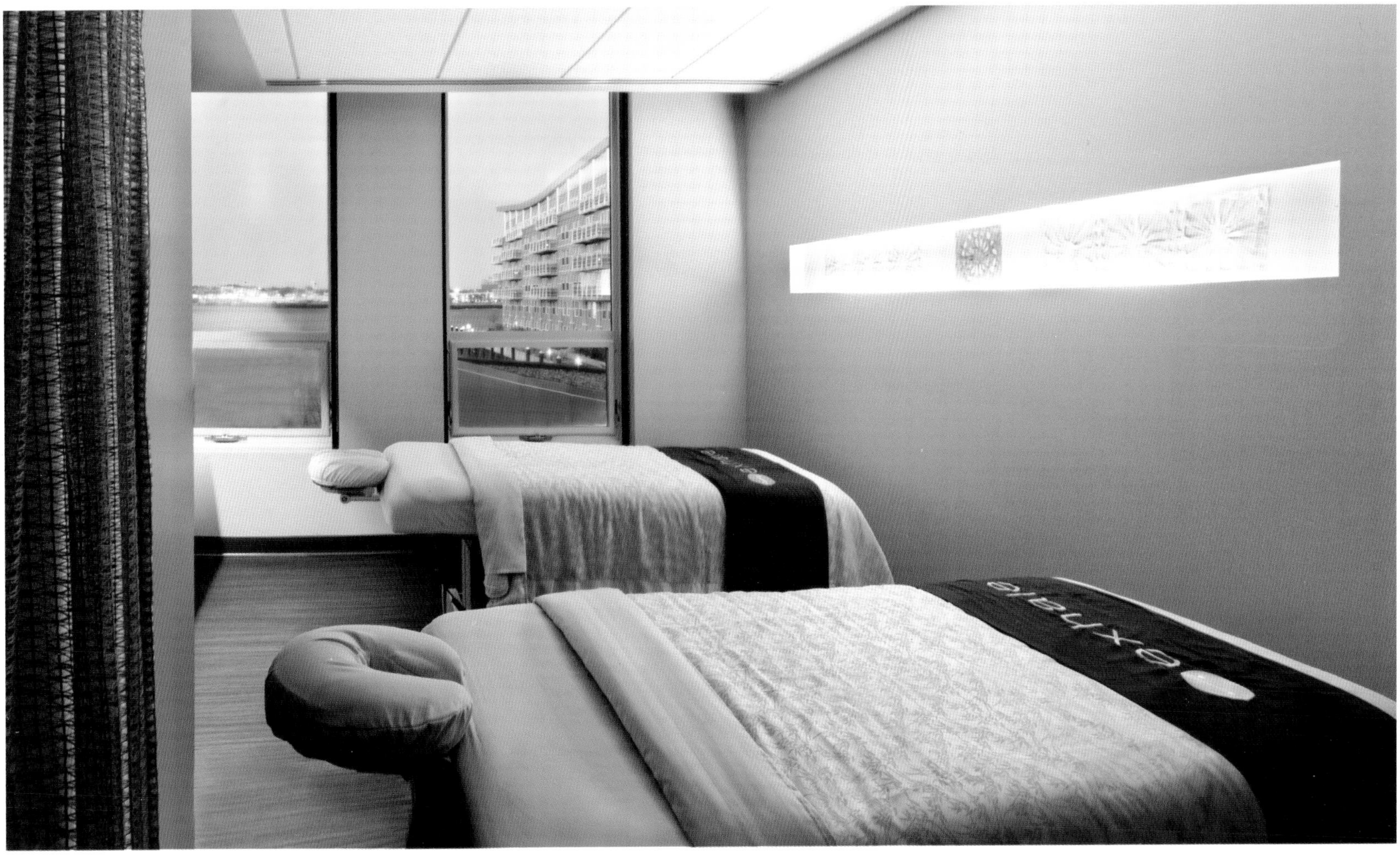

KC Grande Resort & Spa-Hillside

FOS [Foundry of Space]

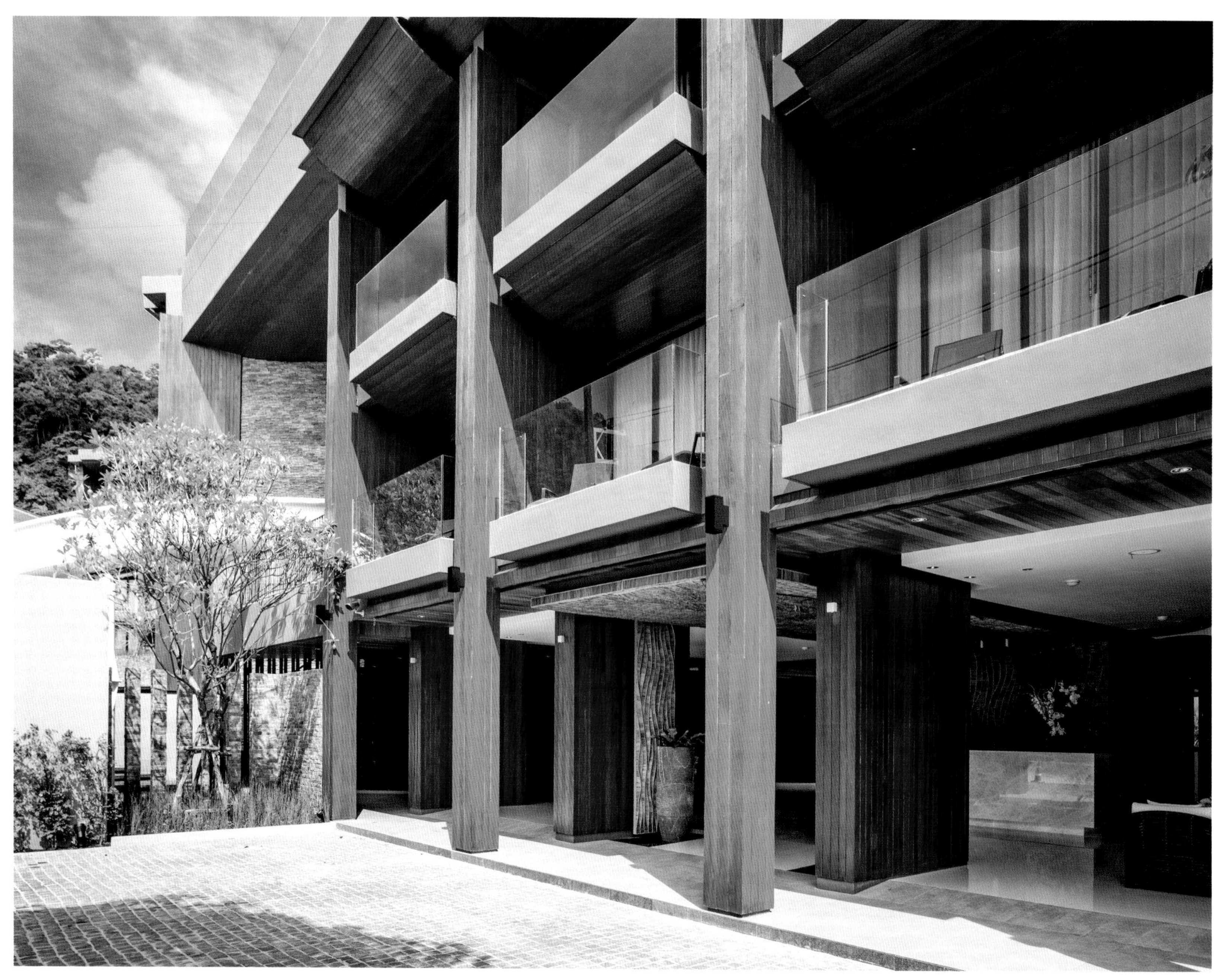

Design Team: Makakrai Jay Suthadarat, Rinchai Chaiwarapon, Singha Ounsakul
Interior Design: Fusionscape [Alisa Tejasrisukko, Thissana Leelahapant]
Structural Engineer: Infra Technology Service
MEP Engineer: Optimum Consultants
Client: Kwan Wattana Co., Ltd.
Location: Koh Chang, Trad, Thailand
Area: 8,000 m^2
Year: 2013
Photography: Teerawat Winyarat

The existing KC Grande Resort & Spa, located on the most beautiful beach in the island: Had Sai Kao (White Sand Beach), has welcomed its guests in full capacity for the last couple years. To accommodate the increasing number of bookings in the near future, the new extension demands additional 79 keys with facilities including pools, a restaurant, bars and sun-bathing decks.

By splitting the building into two parts in two different levels according to the existing topography, we optimize the internal space between the 5-metre different levels of the front and the back buildings while also strategically placing a 30m-long pool and a 3.5m-high artificial waterfall as a focal point in middle of the space. On the first floor of both the lower and upper buildings, all guestrooms have direct access to the plunge pools of their own, representing the effect of being adjacent to the sea. Another advantage of locating the back building on top of the slope is that most of the guestrooms have clear view towards the sea, not being blocked by the lower building and other buildings in front.

On the rooftop level of the lower building, a 40m-long infinity-edge pool with a pool bar at the far end provides a unique experience of being at the seam line between the sky and the horizon overlooking towards Had Sai Khao Beach.

The architectural elements, from the scale of the facade to the interior space of the project, are treated as the performing character of wooden weaving, a local craftsmanship. The interplay of light and shadow is subtly articulated in various part of the building.

Mahash Natural Hair Spa – Moscow

Reis Design

Client: Mahash Salon & Spa
Area: 86 m^2

Reis design created this premium spa & beauty salon for Moscow based salon & spa brand, Mahash.

Mahash Natural Hair Spa comprises: a retail store, hair salon, manicure & pedicure studio &cosmetology Room.

Natural Hair Spa is the second location Reis Design has created for Mahash. The latest store specializes in express hair and beauty services to complement the full day spa experience of the flagship Natural Day Spa.

уход за волосами
стайлинг
AVEDA
color conserve

уход за волосами
стайлинг
уход за
AVEDA
MAHASH

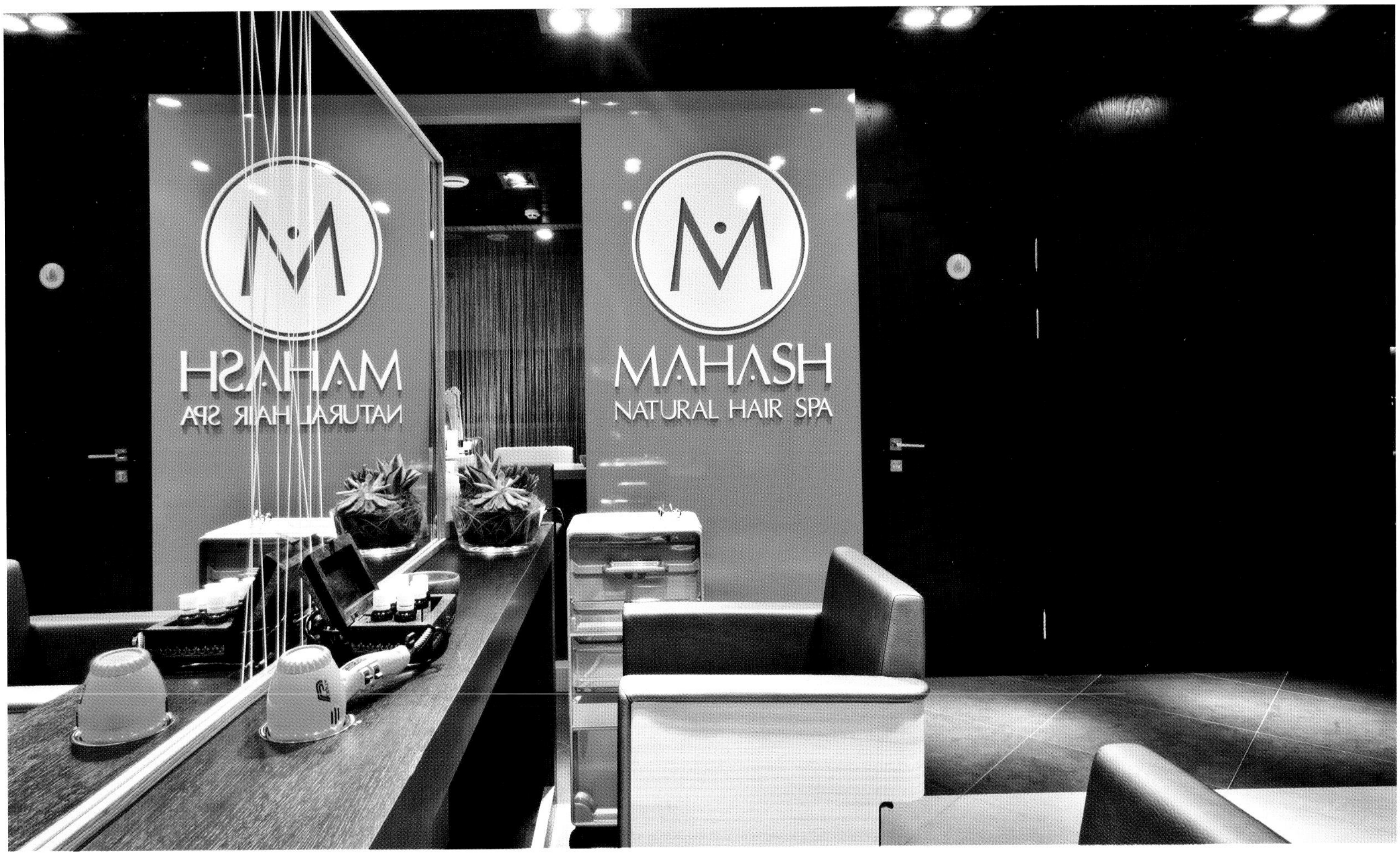
MAHASH
NATURAL HAIR SPA

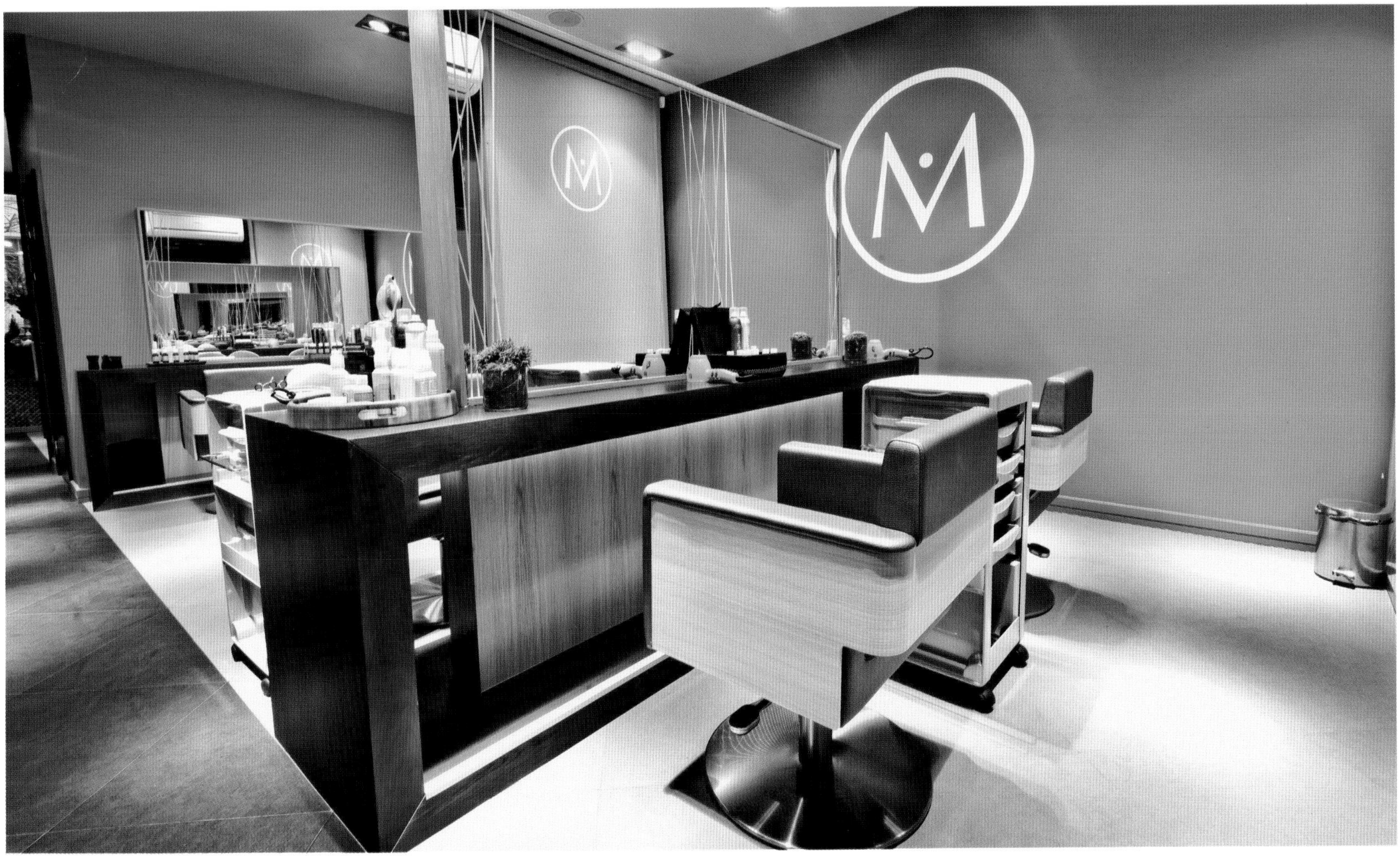

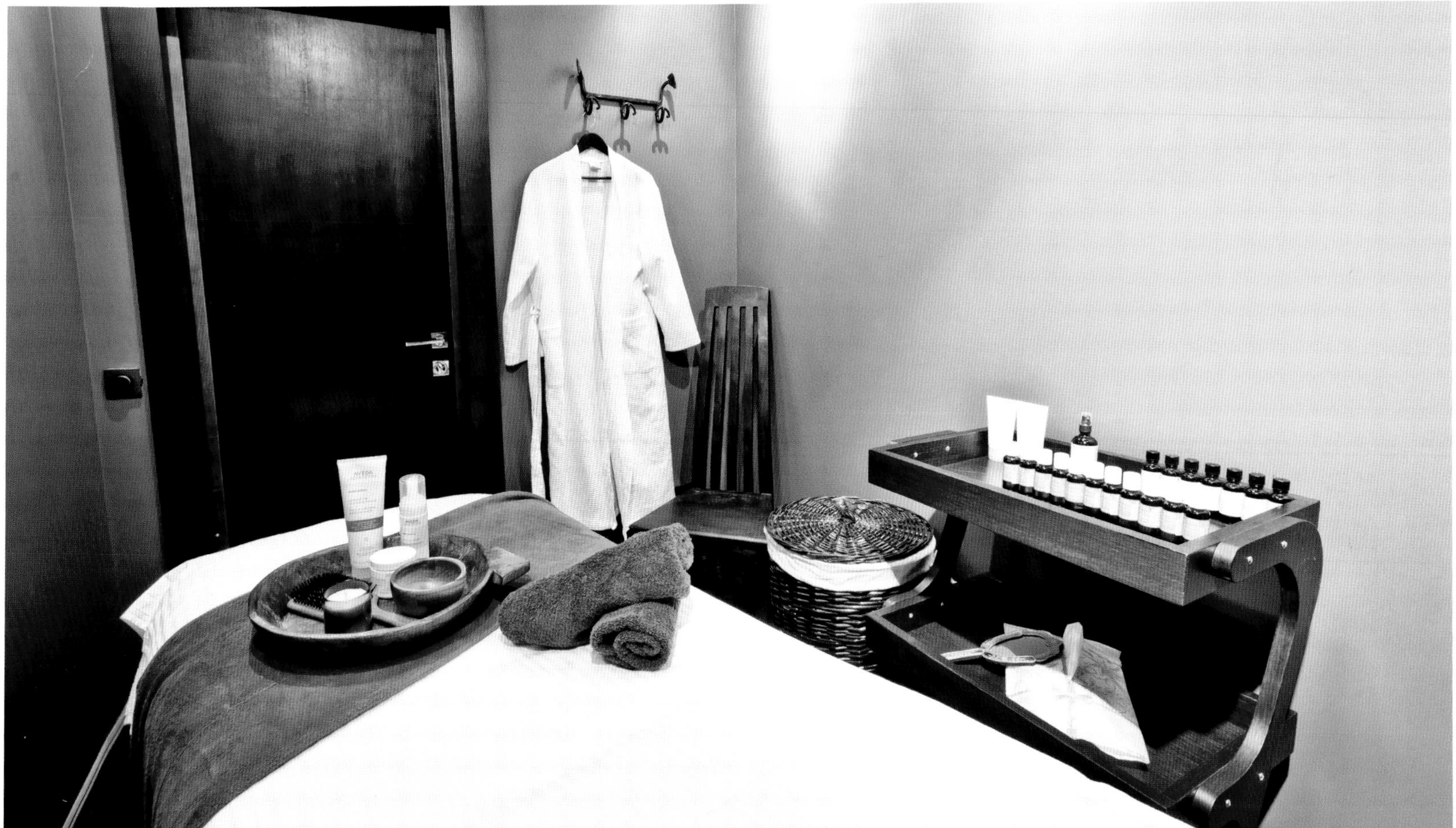

Therme Wien

4a Architekten

Location: Vienna, Austria
Photography: Cathrine Stukhard, Bad Vöslau

Nestling in the spa gardens of Vienna Oberlaa, Austria's largest spa resort invites visitors to enjoy a special relaxing experience with a varied range of pools, rest areas and beauty facilities. The driving force behind the design concept of this new spa resort is nature itself: the central motif is a stream that winds and washes through and around stones, becoming sometimes narrower, sometimes wider. 4a Architekten have succeeded in shaping a unique multisensory bathing landscape with this inspiration in mind. The starting point is one of two thermal springs. The building follows its course in a meandering topographical flow, downwards towards the south, washing over and around individual "theme stones" that project like large river pebbles. The spa ensemble, which reaches three storeys at its highest point, fits in perfectly with its surroundings, and its sunbathing lawns form a gentle transition between the various outdoor pools and the surrounding park. Only the health centre sets a striking signal with its five storeys and dynamic form at the entrance.

The visitor enters via the mouth of the stream, where the foyer is located, and follows the path downstream, past the assorted "theme stones" towards the spring itself. The path widens and narrows, surprising the visitor with different scenarios and perspectives, repeatedly arousing his curiosity as to what might be hiding around the next corner. Bands of light set in places in the flooring relate sympathetically with the motif of the stream. A variety of water attractions create further highlights: sometimes flowing like a gentle curtain down a wall or bubbling and splashing into cascading pools.

site plan

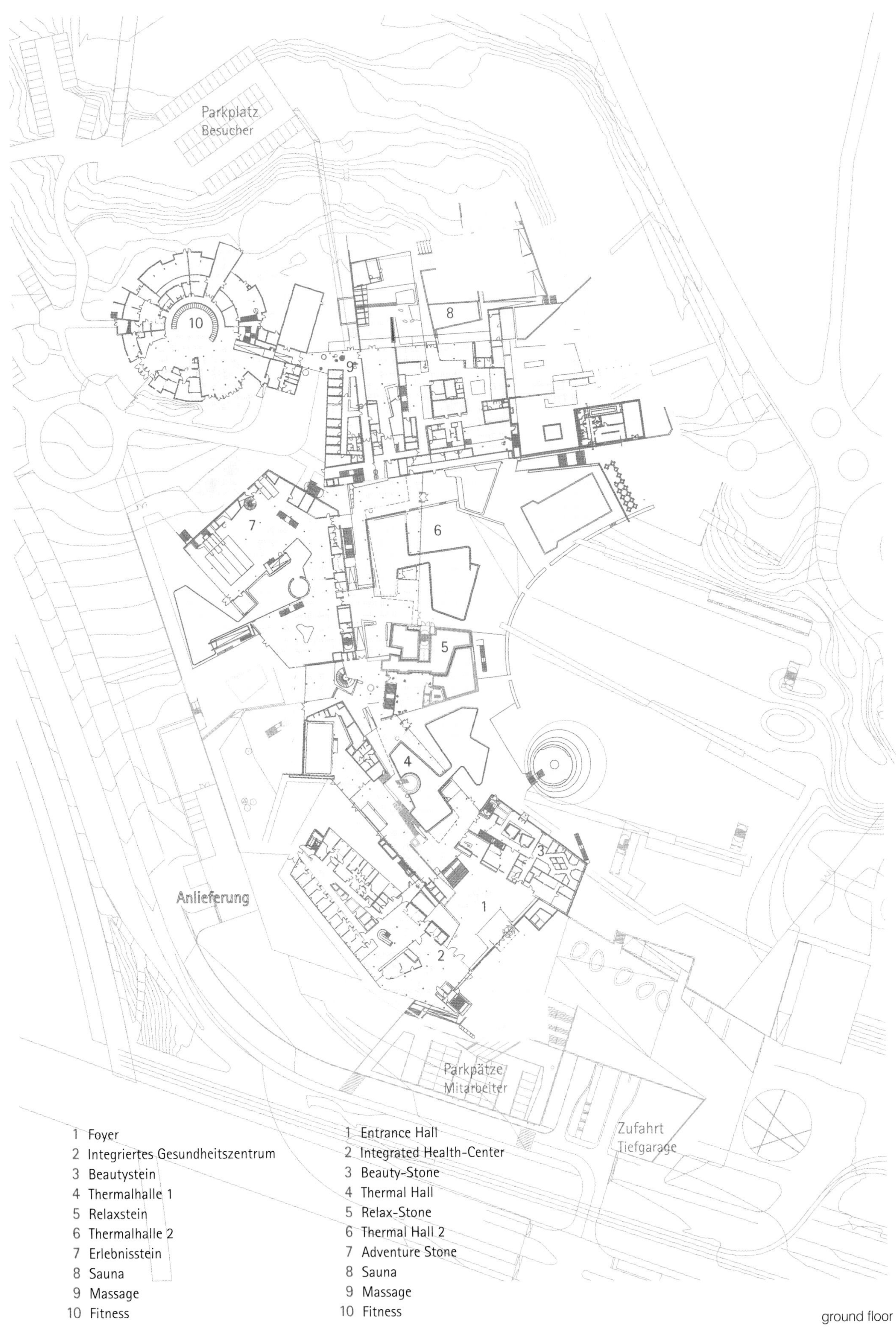

ground floor

Erlebnis Stein

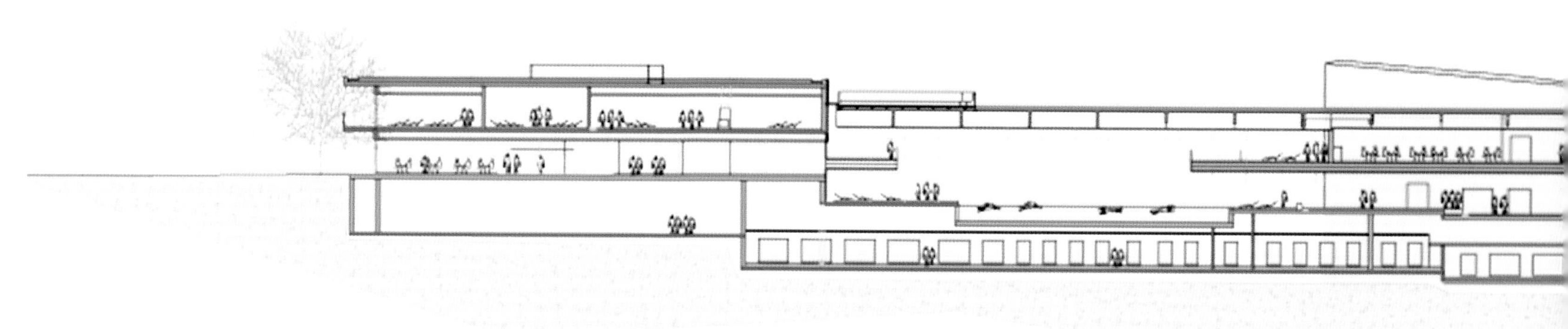

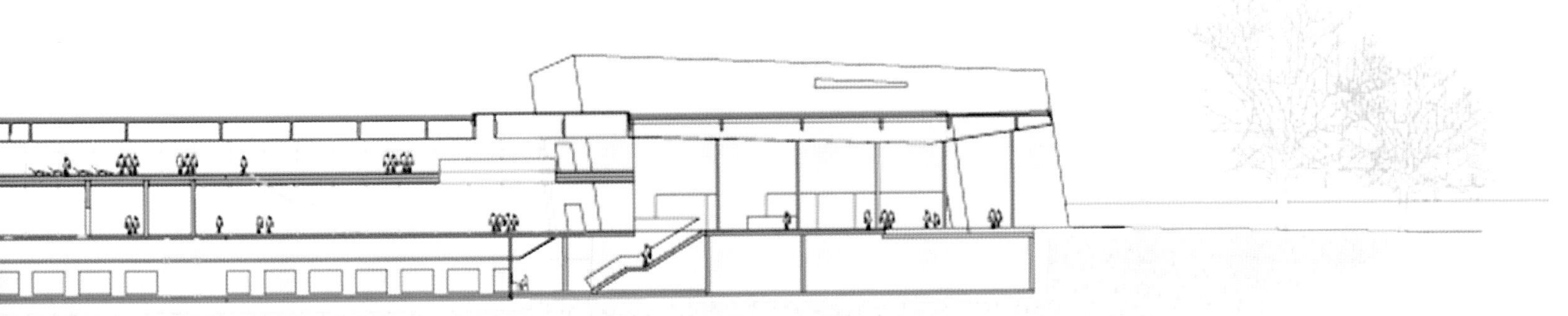

longitudinal section

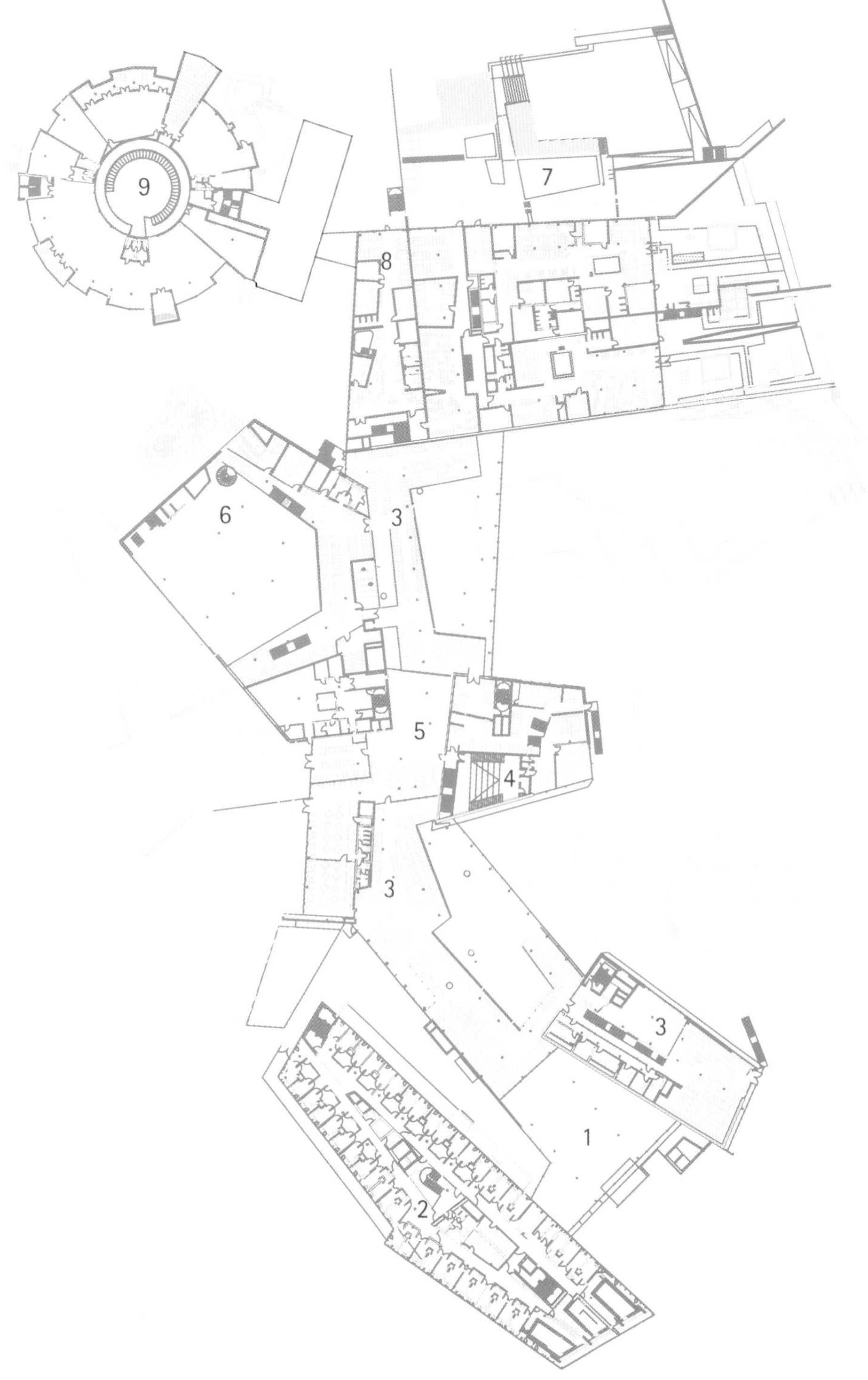

1 Foyer
2 Integriertes Gesundheitszentrum
3 Liegegalerie
4 Kino
5 Restaurant
6 Erlebnisstein
7 Sauna
8 Solesauna
9 Fitness

1 Entrance Hall
2 Integrated Health-Center
3 Gallery
4 Cinema
5 Restaurant
6 Adventure Stone
7 Sauna
8 Brine Sauna
9 Fitness

first floor

4m
3m
1m

4m
3m

Contributor

4a Architekten

The architecture of 4a is characterized by its intense involvement with the emotional effects of space. The aim is to create buildings with a special atmosphere which convey a sense of well-being. Our plans are therefore always geared towards people and their needs. Added to this is the need to create a functional, long-lasting while at the same time aesthetically pleasing building. The basis for this approach is the incorporation of the history and culture of the location together with the requirements of the client and the users of the building. Equally central to the design are an ongoing dialogue and even-handed experimentation with the elements of space, material, colour, light and graphics. By allowing these aspects to guide the design process, individual approaches to a solution can be developed, giving rise to buildings with an independent character without the need to resort to any existing typologies. What results is a coherent concept that does not embody any one given style but which captures in detail the essence and special character of the task in hand.

A2arquitectos

Under the direction of the architects Juan Manzanares Suárez and Cristian Santandreu Utermark, this studio is dedicated to the creation, adaptation, modification and management of architectural and urban planning projects of all kinds.

The studio undertakes building, urban planning, interior design, furniture design, and both renovation and new builds projects. It specializes in projects related to the tourist sector and has carried out numerous projects in different hotels in Spain and France.

A4ESTUDIO

A4estudio was founded in 2004.

An architecture that is understood from the beginning as a platform for personal growth, professional and academic, which considers each request for proposal as an opportunity, contribution and research.

Party with the ultimate goal of rethinking the ways and methods to approach the architectural problem, understanding the development of a project as an intellectual, relational and complex.

Focuses on variables such as structure, program, space and matter of their research axes projective being able to motivate these issues and articulating different lines of action and reflection.

Considered essential in its development to avoid isolation causing critical interactions with other academic and professional development to complement their professional work.

At this time it has developed project work, project executive, technical management, construction management and real estate developments.

Armani Hotel

Giorgio Armani S.p.A., founded in 1975 by Giorgio Armani and Sergio Galeotti, is today one of the world's leading fashion and lifestyle companies. It designs, manufactures, distributes and retails fashion and lifestyle products including apparel, accessories, eyewear, watches, jewellery, fragrances, cosmetics, skincare and home furnishings under a range of labels including Giorgio Armani Privé, Giorgio Armani, Armani Collezioni, Emporio Armani, AJ | Armani Jeans, A | X Armani Exchange, and Armani/Casa.

The Armani Hotels & Resorts division was established by Giorgio Armani S.p.A. in 2005 at its Milan headquarters, where Giorgio Armani himself has been personally directing the design development with a dedicated team.

Banyan Tree

Banyan Tree Hotels and Resortsoffer an intimate retreat experience featuring its signature blend of romance, rejuvenation and exotic sensuality. The first Banyan Tree opened in 1994, transforming an ecological wasteland into an environmentally sensitive resort – our flagship Banyan Tree Phuket, a part of the Laguna Phuket development.

Our philosophy is based on providing a place for rejuvenation of the body, mind and soul - a Sanctuary for the Senses. Placing special emphasis on providing guests with a sense of place, each Banyan Tree property is designed to fit into its natural surroundings, using indigenous materials as far as possible and reflecting the landscape and architecture of the destination.

The brand takes its name from the tropical banyan tree, known for its strong and graceful image. For centuries, the banyan tree has been a symbol of sanctuary under which one finds peace of mind and internal harmony - the same elements upon which Banyan Tree Hotels and Resorts has flourished. Furthermore, the tree shares the same Asian roots as the Banyan Tree group, which is steeped in Asian traditions and environmental consciousness.

Pioneering the tropical garden spa concept with Asian health and beauty remedies passed down from generations, Banyan Tree Spa was created as the signature experience in all Banyan Tree resorts, to complement the "Sanctuary for the Senses" wellness concept. With the emphasis on high service standards and consistency, therapists are professionally trained at Banyan Tree Spa Academies in Phuket, Thailand, and Lijiang, China. An award-winning international spa brand, Banyan Tree Spa introduced innovative spa concepts such as the Rainmist experience, The Rainforest hydrothermal concept and Master Therapist Experience.

The Banyan Tree Gallery supports local communities by exhibiting and retailing indigenous handicrafts, which are also found in the resorts. A quintessential highlight of the Banyan Tree experience, Banyan Tree Gallery aspires to recreate the unique Banyan Tree experience with its extensive selection of Asian-style furnishings, Banyan Tree Spa collection, eco-friendly products, indigenous village handicrafts, ethnic apparel and accessories, and objects d'art.

To date, the Banyan Tree Group manages and/or has ownership interests in close to 30 resorts and hotels, over 60 spas, and 80 retail galleries; as well as three golf courses.

====================================

Concrete

GONZALEZ & JACOBSON ARCHITECTURE, S. L. is a dream factory. Located at the elegant urbanization of Marbella, Hacienda Las Chapas, for more than twenty successful years and which combines creativity with professionalism, international experience with a deep knowledge of current market needs. More than a company is a family of multidisciplinary experts, up to sixteen people, including architects, designers and drafters, who are dedicated in creating projects where quality has become an emblem and perfection in goal.

====================================

De Jorio Design International

De Jorio Design International is a leading Italian architecture and design company, created in 1956 by the architect Giuseppe de Jorio. From the 80's joined the studio Vittorio de Jorio and Marco de Jorio introducing new mind and new ideas following directly all the new projects. Since the very beginning, its activity has been centered on the civil, both public and private, and ship building fields. But it is in designing Passenger and Cruise Vessels that De Jorio Design has really built its history. In the last 50 years Giuseppe de Jorio and his company have been the consultants for the most important Italian passenger ship and cruise ferry owners and shipyards. Moreover, the company has acquired considerable experience in the designing of luxury mega yachts. It is in the naval field that the company has been most successful and up to today it has signed more than 200 projects in 50 years of activity. The team of the studio is made up of architects and interior and graphic designers. The board is made up of chairman Giuseppe de Jorio and founding partners Vittorio and Marco de Jorio.

Style

The Studio's design is based on a balanced planning lay-out and an architectonic development of the environments, differentiated in their themes, but sufficiently homogeneous in their expressive forms, obtained from a search for absolute elegance in terms of space, shapes and lines joined by the perfect harmonization of colors and materials. Despite their presence worldwide, being Italians, living and working in Italy that has always been the birthplace of all arts, makes up in its own right a cultural heritage that is without equal, a source of inspiration for design also when they propose projects with a feeling different from European models. The result is a design of "Italian" taste.

====================================

dwp

design worldwide partnership (dwp) is an integrated design consultancy with over 2,500 completed projects and 500 professionals delivering services in;

- Architecture
- Interior Design
- Graphic Design
- Facility Planning
- Project Management
- Feasibility Studies and
- Turn Key Design and Construction.

dwp strives for design excellence through creativity and innovation. This is reflected in our globally recognized and award winning projects. Our core values inspire our designers to embrace design challenges and surpass client's expectations.

At dwp we use our global diversity to deliver an exceptional and unique level of service. Where ever we operate we want to be seen as the leading multi-cultural design company that works in collaboration to deliver simply the best design.

====================================

FZI Interiors

Born in 2006 in Milan with the aim to develop the set design for theatre and cinema, FZI Interiors applies its techniques to the architecture field, particularly in the hotel interior design. Scene and interior designers coming from a wide experience in theatre and cinema, Elisabetta Frazuoli and Francesca Fezzi are able to think original and tailored solutions for any kind of space, from a show room to a private house, from the room of a hotel to its spa. The starting point of the design project is always a base concept: FZI experts imagine the room internal spaces as a living scene with the eyes of the set designer, skilled to create a truthful ambience. The creative solutions include traditional and new materials, in order to integrate the realization style with the imagination also, minding that beauty is always oriented to functionality, to time schedule and budget.

====================================

FOUNDRY OF SPACE

FOUNDRY OF SPACE is a Bangkok-based design office practicing architecture and urbanism.

We position ourselves at the convergence between architects and cultural analysts where socio-economic, political, environmental and other relevant factors are among our key design parameters.

FOS's fascination is primarily focused on contents and context of each project.

Through our comprehensive research in building programmes and transformation process towards logically innovative design, we believe that our architecture is not only able to enhance quality of built environment for people to live in, but also to inspire whoever works, plays, rests or has any kind of experiences with our architecture.

Simultaneously, FOS consistently strives for mutual permeation between architecture and its urban fabric in order to stimulate the constructive coexistence between the new contents and the existing context.

==================================

HBA

Inge Moore is Principle, HBA International Hirsch Bedner Associates London. Inge studied and began her career in South Africa and has completed work for both commercial and non-commercial industries. Her experience in interior design includes complete project management including concept, planning, presentations; selection and specification as well as the design of bespoke pieces specifically produced for each project; through to final procurement, management and on-site installation.

K. Michelle Evans is Managing Associate/Senior Project Designer in Hirsch Bedner Associates. Michelle is a professional with over 20 years of experience in design and construction including 16 years in International Projects. She Specializes in the leisure and hospitality sector and is actively involved in the designs of hotels, restaurants and clubs in the U.K, The United States, Singapore, Zimbabwe, Borneo, India, Bermuda, Maldives and Japan. Michelle has a full range of abilities from preliminary programming and conceptual design through space planning, design development, selection and specification of finishes & FF&E, construction documentation with AutoCAD, and drawing coordination with other consultants.

==================================

Igloodgn

Igloo design is a dynamic firm on the forefront of cutting-edge interior design and branding. Based out of Montreal, the company is internationally renowned for creating innovative spaces, from hotels, restaurants and retail projects, to residential and condominium design. With a focus on designing for profitable businesses, the firm's branding, graphic design and interior design concepts foster advocacy, and ultimately, result in increased lucrative customer experiences.

Established in 2005 by award-winning interior designers Alain Courchesne and Anna Abbruzzo, Igloo design has an illustrious international roster of projects. Both designers bring an unprecedented passion and fresh approach to design, focusing on building a detailed brand identity in each project from inception to completion.

Deeply rooted in distinguishing the overall experience and essence of a brand, Igloo design creates a space while simultaneously establishing its identity. All elements of an experience must be in harmony with one another from branding to interior design to custom furniture design. At Igloo design, excellence can only be reached by a combination of disciplines that collaborate to create a well-balanced entity.

==================================

Irina Samoylova

My name is Irina Samoylova I'm 25 years old, I live in Saint Petersburg.

I have strong academic artistic skills, in particular for drawing. My studies in this field started during the period 1998 - 2007 when I graduate at the "Art school and college of Perm" with honors. In 2010 I graduated at the University of Industrial Design in Perm.

For the last five years I have been developing architecture and interior design projects for several customers in Russia: Saint Petersburg, Perm, Samara, Omsk, and Yekaterinburg.

I am the finalist of international competitions in industrial design and architecture: "Jump the Gap" - 2011, where I have participated at the competition submitting my project "Live Bath Anemone"

2011 James Dyson award - national finalist: project name MISTY GARDEN

2011/2012 Master of Interior Design, IED Milano - winner of scholarships

==================================

JOSIF MILENKOVIC

Josif Milenkovic is the member of Serbian Chamber of Engineers (part of European Council of Engineers Chambers), Licence 300 (Responsible Designer for Architectural Projects).

He is design project leader of "Sport and recreational hotel complex Pasha's Fountain", Serbia, since 2010. He works on conceptual urban project, Ras Al Khaimah tourist resort, UAE, hotel project and interior design, Ras Al Khaimah, UAE, city planing projects, project "Bagat", Leskovac, Serbia and various residential and public building projects.

==================================

Khosla Associates

Khosla Associates is a leading Architecture and Interior Design firm in Bangalore India. The Principal Architect, MD and founder, Sandeep Khosla, studied architecture at Pratt Institute, New York and returned to India to establish Khosla Associates in 1995.

The team at Khosla Associates, headed by Sandeep Khosla and Director, Amaresh Anand consists of highly driven design professionals who create a versatile body of work ranging from architecture and interiors of residences and corporate offices to retail and hospitality spaces.

Khosla Associate's distinct style of tropical residential architecture uses local materials and concepts, but reinterprets them with an innovative and contemporary design sensibility. The firm's interest in global/local trends in fashion, lifestyle and design is reflected in their varied palette of interior projects ranging from corporate offices for Nike, ING Vysya, and MTV amongst others, to lounge bars and restaurants around the country such as Shiro, Spinn, Touch and Roxy. Khosla Associates have also made significant impact in the retail sphere in India by redefining new looks for major brands such as Hard Rock Café, Café Coffee Day, KFC, Pizza Hut, Wrangler, and Ritu Kumar and have designed a significant traveling exhibition called Global Local for the British Council.

==================================

plajer & franz studio

In over a decade of creative and imaginative partnership, plajer & franz studio, founded in 1996 by architects alexander plajer & werner franz, has built up an impressively broad-ranging portfolio with an international client base. the development of brand architecture and corporate identity in retail as well as the design of premium hotels and resorts form the core of their expertise. plajer & franz studio has an international reputation for innovative excellence, quality down to the smallest detail, great planning skills and a superb sense of style. From private yacht to automobile trade stand via award-winning bars and luxury hotels, the key to plajer & franz studio's freshness of vision lies in their continuous exploration and cross-fertilisation between disciplines and areas of experience. our ability to deliver show-stoppingly innovative design with elegant and meticulous finishing down to the smallest detail lies in being able to take what we learn in one area and applying it, where appropriate, in another: high tech material forming from the car industry, for example, may yield exciting new surfaces for a shop-in-shop project, whereas new developments in the use of digital display techniques from the bar and club scene might fit perfectly with a new automobile display concept – it's all in the mix!

==================================

PRVS GROUP

Architect and Art/Design master, Alessio Patalocco (1982), graduated at Rome Architecture University. After some important collaborations (including Massimiliano Fuksas Studio), he opens his Art , Archirecture and Design Studio in Terni, Italy in 2009.He's assisting History chair in "Roma Tre" Architecture University (from 2007) and doctor in research (from 2010) in the Department for Project and Analysis of Architecture in the same university (Urban Sustainable Project section). He won several important architecture contests with the group PRVS (of which he's the cofounder); we can mention for exemple the brand new Magliano Sabina "ecological bridge" (Italy) , and the contest for the new airport of Gui Lin (China) as planning advisor for ADR and CACC engineering groups. As ADR engineering planning advisor and in association with PVRS , Alessio Patalocco also won the second prize in the new Xianmeng and Chengzhou airport project contest of China. Several local showrooms published his artistic creations and his works , as far as his interventions, had been published in several magazines and books.

==================================

Reis Design

Reis Design was founded in 2004 with the purpose of providing good value, innovative & commercially successful design for Branded Retail environments.

We are a small company, with a passion for quality & obsessive attention to detail, dedicated to providing a reliable, personal service to our clients.

We have continued to build on-going relationships with a variety of global brands and retailers on high profile projects ranging in scale from promotional sites & retail concessions to large scale store design & development. We have forged long standing relationships with a variety of dedicated contractors & crafts people around the UK & Europe, enabling us to provide a turnkey service, taking your project from the initial creative design process to planning & site construction.

Our commitment to creative design and professional management ensures that our ideas are translated into successful projects, which work both aesthetically and commercially

==================================

Richmond International

Over 40 years ago we set the benchmark for international hospitality design, and have been at the forefront ever since. We believe intelligent design can bring life to each and every individual space, allowing global brands to deliver out-standing world-class experiences. We are cultured in the art of "designing hospitality".

==================================

S3 Design

S3 Design is a full service architectural, planning and design firm with a specific focus on athletics, recreation, fitness, and wellness. S3 Design's practice is dedicated to creating spaces that increase the users well being and athletic performance. S3's work ranges from Athletic and Recreation Centers for Colleges and Universities to spa's and fitness centers for private owners. S3 Design believes that the architectural experience can positively impact how a client, member, or user interacts with a space, thus encouraging them to continue returning to an environment that betters their well being.

==================================

Sid Lee Architecture

Founded in 2009 following the integration of architecture firm NOMADE (founded in 1999), Sid Lee Architecture is a partnership between seasoned architects and urban designers Jean Pelland and Martin Leblanc, and Sid Lee, a global commercial creativity company. Established in Montreal, with satellite offices in Amsterdam (Netherlands) and Paris (France), Sid Lee Architecture boasts a team of 25 architects, technicians, designers, managers and support personnel. This multidisciplinary team enjoys a solid reputation, having successfully carried out many large-scale projects. Sharing common views on interior design, brand strategy, urban approach, and the role of context, the Sid Lee Architecture team has had the opportunity to put its knowledge and expertise to work, successfully completing a wide range of multidisciplinary projects.

==================================

Silvia Giannini Architetto

Graduated at University of Architecture in Florence, Silvia Giannini is specialized in Spa and Wellness design.

Her work is related to hotels and Spa, in different meanings: Urban or Hotel Spa, Fitness Centers, valorization and innovation of mineral spring Spa product.

Her professional path is directed to atmospheres, shapes, objects, in order to the specific identity of every project trough a technical knowledge, based on the singular project and its management.

Her target is giving a soul to the paces, using architecture as a filter. Spaces are expression of people who wanted them, or their intentions; space as transfer to the customers of the emotions for what tit has been created for.

Essential concept, rarefied atmosphere, soft lights, fabrics and roundness, and comforts.

About this concepts, she has carried out masters and hold specific speech in national and international conferences.

==================================

Simone Micheli

Simone Micheli founded the architectural studio having his name in 1990 and the Design Company named "Simone Micheli Architectural Hero" in 2003. Professor at the University, in particular at the Polidesign and the Scuola Politecnica di Design in Milan. He exhibited his works at the Venice Biennale, in the architectural sector. He works as editor of the theme exhibition named "contract" as well of the major international exhibitions in this field.

He represents the Italian interior design at the "XXX Colombian Architecture Convention" at Barranquilla, Colombia and in 2008 he attended the International Architecture Convention in Hannover, Germany, for the contracting. The "La Casa Italiana" exhibition taking place at the São Paulo (Brazil) "Mube" sculpture museum in 2008 and in Mexico City and in Monterrey in 2009 bears his name.

His professional activity moves in different directions: from architecture to interior design, from design to visual design going throught mass-media and social media; his creations, ecofriendly and oriented to nature, are defined by a strong identity and uniqueness. His architectural making is enriched by various creations for public administrations and for important private committents.

All the works by Architect Simone Micheli are unique and feature a strong personality in addition to being sustainable, environmental friendly. He plays a crucial role in the planning field in Europe, in fact he developed a number of plans for public administration and for prestigious customers related to the community and to the residence field. A number of monographs and international magazines focused on his works are available.

==================================

Studio 92

Studio92 is a renowned architecture, planning, engineering and interior design firm with almost 20 years of experience. In recent years has worked on some of the Croatian largest projects in turist industry and SPA business.

Our design team made of architect , enginears and designesr can offer specialist services or a fully integrated design service to satisfy all our clients needs. Our design philosophy revolves around a goal to create spaces of lasting aesthetic quality and functionality. We try to design spaces that capture the imagination and move the emotions.

==================================

Studio Alberto Apostoli

Alberto Apostoli was born in Verona in 1968. Graduated in Industrial Electronics, degree in architecture in Venice in 1993 with a thesis about Economy. He opens in 1997, Apostoli & Associati Studio, characterized by a varied professional vocation consequence of its personal path. In 2006 opens its first personal exhibition at the headquarters of the European Parliament in Brussels by the title "contaminated architectures between communication and design", causing the attention of the European press. In the same year he opens a study in Guangzhou (China) and in 2007 a representative office in Casablanca. Alberto Apostoli has design and marketing culture, that gives every project strong innovation. His projects are published all over the world. Takes conferences, courses and workshops in Italy and abroad on different areas of design.

==================================

Studio Bizzarro & Partners

The Studio Bizzarro & Partners achieved, in Italy, in more than 20 years, a specific experience in consulting and design of structures for hospitality and wellness, according to the Italian Style, creating projects that aim to make people live emotional and sensorial experiences, memorable and extraordinary.

The studio has designed many hotels and resorts' projects, with the intent of giving a pleasant staying in prestige environments, with an innovative and refined design.

Spa, thermae, beauty farm and wellness centres where the water itself is not only intended as an healing element, but most of all as a real fun, relax and source of emotions.

Wellness clubs and implants for physical activity that join to an excellent logistic, a refined technology and utilizations of an effective and profitably space.

Buildings still inspired to design criteria that put at the centre of every environment the research of a lifestyle aimed on wellness.

==================================

Studio Matteo Nunziati

Matteo Nunziati opened his interior design office in Milan in 2000.

The product design department of the studio collaborates with some of the most important furniture, lighting and covering firms.

The department of tnterior design is specialized in designing luxury hotels, residences and privat villas, wellness centers and spas, which have been constructed all over the world.

==================================

Thermarium Baeder-Bau GmbH

Thermarium was founded in 1997 and is one of the world's leading suppliers of spa services and products. It provides A to Z solutions that include consulting, feasibility studies, architectural design and engineering, custom-made spa products and spa management. The company is recognised as a pioneering force in spa design, installing high-specification wellness facilities across the globe. The company´s spa consulting department brings together local economic and operational resources with the latest technology for each of its projects.

==================================

Tom Hisano

TOMS & DESIGN ASSOCIATES LTD. was founded in Hong Kong SAR in 2000, and opened branch office in Hanoi, Vietnam in 2007.

Founder, Tom Hisano, has been a professional interior designer and only Japanese professional at Hong Kong Interior Design Association in 2011. His design works have been published in several interior magazines throughout Asia and an invited speaker at International Design Conference like HA+DEXPO, 2010. His Philosophy is "Givers' Gain" His motto is "Good Design is good for Business and Future" His mission is to create master plan for Commercial/Hospitality Architecture and Interior Spaces in Asia – such as Residential project, Villa, Hotel, Serviced Apartment, Club House, Beauty Saloon & SPA, Restaurant, Bar, Kids School, Elderly Home & Commercial Projects. He has been located in Japan, Hong Kong, China, Vietnam and Cambodia and more in Asia.

Member Bio: Tom Hisano is Managing & Creative Director of the company. He had been Chief Representative of PANASONIC, Japan in Hong Kong from 1989 to 1994. He studied interior design in Osaka, Japan after graduation of management master degree at University in Kyushu in Japan and has been a professional member of Interior Design Association in Hong Kong from 2007.

==================================

Viceroy

In skyscraping cities and pacesetting playgrounds, Viceroy Hotels and Resorts embody the essence of style and service.

Expansive oceanfront villas in Anguilla, Zihuatanejo, and Riviera Maya, exclusive cosmopolitan suites in Miami, slopeside retreats in Snowmass and sunny enclaves in Palm Springs and Santa Monica: experience surroundings that inspire discerning guests to indulge in a life as singular as it is sumptuous. And as the year unfolds, discover the collection's first resorts beyond the Americas: the recent additions of Yas Viceroy Abu Dhabi and Viceroy Maldives in the Indian Ocean, and the future introductions of Viceroy Istanbul and Viceroy Bodrum in Turkey.

==================================

Zhou Shaoyu

Zhou Shaoyu, the national registered associate constructor, engineer, registered interior designer, member of the 8th Professional Committee under China Institute of Interior Design (CIID), the general manager and design director of Fuzhou Zicheng Decoration Engineering Co., Ltd.

He was awarded the Jintang Prize in the 2011 China-Designer Interior Design Annual Selection for Top Ten Leisure Space, Merit Award in 2nd China International Space Environment Art Design Competition Nest Award, Shortlisted in 2011 Idea-Tops International Space Design Competition, and the 2nd Prize in 2011-2012 International Environmental Art Innovation Design (Huading Award) of Commercial Space Section.

==================================

ENOTA

"Constant changes and new complex situations in the world around us drive us to think about new ways of architectural and urban organizations. In order to be able to produce answers to those new questions we believe it's time to surpass the boundaries of conventional discipline set mainly by our cultural backgrounds. ENOTA's team of architects focuses on research driven design of the environment where study of contemporary social organizations and use of new technologies are interwoven to produce innovative and effective solutions. ENOTA's solutions are strongly influenced by research, reinterpretation and development of social, organizational and design algorithms that derive from nature. The result is always a strong binding of the buildings with the environment that surrounds them."

ENOTA was founded in 1998 with the ambition to create contemporary and critical architectural practice of an open type based on collective approach to development of architectural and urban solutions. Over the years ENOTA has been constantly developing and from its beginnings it has served as creative platform for more than fifty architects. ENOTA is led by founding partners and principal architects Dean Lah and Milan Tomac.

For their work ENOTA received several national and international architecture awards. Their work has been presented on numerous exhibitions and published in professional and broad interest publications all over the world. ENOTA's principals lecture at architectural schools, conferences and symposiums in Slovenia and abroad.

ENOTA's projects vary from residential and office buildings to cultural, leisure and sports facilities. Main realizations include Ptuj Performance Center (2013), Stambolžioski Dental Studio (2011), Podčetrtek Sports Hall (2010), Wellness Orhidelia (2009), Gruškovje Border Shop (2009), Ilirska Apartments (2008), Terme Tuhelj Spa Resort (2007), Jurčkova Housing (2007), Hotel Sotelia (2006), Wellness Centre Termalija (2004), NKBM Bank Branch (2002), Kraški zidar Headquarters (2002, with A. Dekleva).

==================================